MYTH

Key Concepts in Religion

Also available from Continuum *Key Concepts in Philosophy*:

Myth

Key Concepts in Religion

Robert Ellwood

continuum

Continuum International Publishing Group
The Tower Building
11 York Road
London
SE1 7NX

80 Maiden Lane
Suite 704
New York
NY 10038

www.continuumbooks.com

© Robert Ellwood 2008

British Library Cataloguing-in-Publication Data
A catalogue record for this book is available from the British Library.

ISBN: HB: 1-8470-6234-2
        978-1-8470-6234-5

PB: 1-8470-6235-0
        978-1-8470-6235-2

Library of Congress Cataloguing-in-Publication Data
A catalog record for this book is available from the Library of Congress.

Typeset by Servis Filmsetting Ltd, Stockport, Cheshire
Printed and bound in Great Britain by MPG Books Ltd, Bodmin, Cornwall

CONTENTS

CHAPTER 1

THE OTHER WITHIN: ENCOUNTERING MYTH

DEFINITIONS

Let's start with a definition of myth. Here's one, together with some basic statements about the subject. As you read this book, think about how useful this preliminary definition seems to be. Perhaps you will come up with a better one of your own.

A myth is a story of gods, heroes, or other exceptional beings, usually set in primordial times or in an alternative world, which establishes in narrative form the basic worldview and values of a society. It sets forth the origin, meaning, and practice of the society's organization, rituals, and codes of behavior. Myths include (1) accounts of creation and origins, on the grounds that to know what something really is, or how it is to be done, we need to know where it came from; (2) foundational social myths, such as those establishing kingship, gender roles, etc., usually from a generation soon after the beginning; (3) hero myths, whether of warriors or saviors, that exemplify the defeat of evil and the way back to original right relationships between the ideal and the real in self and world; (4) myths of the ultimate destiny of individual life and of the world; (5) myths that serve to warn against bad behavior; and (6) myths explaining the essential rituals, pilgrimages, and other religious practices of the society.

Under the influence of modern psychological interpretations, the meaning of myth has been more and more individualized, so that myths are taken to serve as individual, or subgroup, models of role, behavior, attitude, and ideal self, rather than serving as important narratives for a large society as a whole.

Myths tend to be the kind of stories that deal with such basic themes in such a dramatic way that one can read or listen to them over and over. Take the following example.

A STORY OF THE BEGINNING

Long ago, when the world had not yet taken its final form, two curious young gods peeked down from the High Plain of Heaven over the area where the islands of Japan now break the surface of the sea. They saw nothing but endless water or floating formless bits of land in all directions. However, one of them, the male Izanagi, held a long spear given him by an older deity. Under instruction from the senior gods, Izanagi and his female companion, Izanami, made their way down the Floating Bridge of Heaven, the Rainbow, to get closer to those endlessly tossing waves. Then, as soon as he could reach them, Izanagi thrust his spear into the foam and churned it around. To their amazement, the liquid solidified until an island formed on which they could stand. The god and goddess descended the rest of the way and, on their tiny private world, erected a pillar and built a palace in which to dwell.

They then began to feel desire for one another. Izanami invited her consort to conjoin with her, devising a ritual by which they would circle the sacred pillar in opposite directions until they met. But the child who was the fruit of this union was weak and mal-formed. Troubled, the couple ascended back up to heaven to consult the senior gods, who determined by divination that the tragic birth was because Izanami had spoken before her husband. The two descended to their island again, and this time did it right. Indeed, in an orgy of procreation the primal pair begat the islands of Japan, together with countless *kami* or gods to inhabit them: *kami* of wind, mountains, trees, rivers, and finally of rice for their sustenance.

But disaster again struck. When Izanami gave birth to the fire-god she was terribly burned; dying, the first earthly mother was com-pelled to go to Yomi, the underworld. Izanagi, overcome by grief, threw himself on the ground and wailed bitterly. Finally he deter-mined to go himself to the realm of the dead and try to bring her back. By the time he found her it was too late; his wife had already eaten of the food of the underworld and thus could never return to the land of the living, like Persephone in the Greek myth of her abduction by Hades; Izanami remonstrated with her consort for his tardiness in coming. Still sorrowing and now full of anger as well, Izanagi retraced his steps, pursued by infernal demons and hags.

The crisis did not auger well for the primal parents' marriage. At the boundary of the underworld, Izanagi declared he would divorce Izanami; she screamed back in retaliation that if he did so she would then bring 1,000 inhabitants of the world down to her realm every day. Furious, he responded he would give life to 1,500 with every sunrise. So it was that death came, but life flourishes nonetheless, bringing more living beings into existence than death can destroy.

Izanagi washed in the ocean to purify himself from the realm of the dead's pollution. Even more gods were born of this process. From the washings of his right eye came Tsukiyomi, god of the moon; from his left eye came Amaterasu, lovely goddess associated with the sun, and to be ancestress of the Japanese imperial line; from his nose came Susanoo, rampaging god of storms, but who was also capable of gentler moments. Of these deities still more tales are told.[1]

This is the story of creation found in ancient Japanese texts. It is an example of the kind of story commonly termed a myth. Myth, like religion, is difficult to define exactly. To be sure, stories called myths have a peculiar feel about them – archaic, often bizarre and cruel, yet also haunting – but what is it precisely that they say and do?

UNDERSTANDING MYTH

In thinking about that question, let us first consider conventional scholarly conceptions of myth.[2] A myth is usually defined as a "traditional story" – that is, one that has been handed down for as long as anyone can remember. No one knows who wrote myths; in fact, they probably go back before the invention of writing. They must have had their beginning in story-telling, perhaps around a campfire or during long dark nights in winter quarters, and were transmitted orally for many generations before being set down by scribes.

We need to take a moment to consider how important story-telling was before writing. We may now think of telling stories as a relatively secondary aspect of civilization, appropriate for children or for entertainment, but not the way absolutely crucial knowledge or life-skills are transmitted; that involves reading: in books and journals, or now perhaps on the internet. But think what it was like before there was anything to read. Absolutely everything conveyed in words had to be memorized, and then told by word of mouth. The bard was what the printing press is now.

Sometimes, of course, laws, directions, and the like could be given in flat statements. But bards quickly realized that the lore of a tribe is far more grippingly portrayed, and far more easily remembered both by teller and hearer, if it is told through a story. It is even better if the story is in the form of epic verse, in which meter, rhyming words, and alliteration make remembering long passages still easier to hold in mind, and which can cast a spell drawing listeners ever more deeply into the tale: thus the Iliad and Odyssey of Homer, the sagas of the Norsemen, and many more such poetic narratives.

So it was that these stories before writing not only entertained, or even just passed on such interesting but perhaps esoteric-seeming information as the origin of the world, and what lies beyond the frontiers of the world as we know it. In the process they also showed how society is properly organized, with its leaders and priests, and why; how a husband and wife, a parent and child, should act (or not act) one to another; how a warrior or hunter behaves and what his values are; what is taboo, and what places and times are sacred; what the names and qualities of the various animals and geographical locations roundabout are; and what characterizes the various peoples, friend and foe, one is likely to encounter. Like Australian Aboriginals following their "songlines," one could sometimes travel hundreds, even thousands, of miles on land or sea using only a good myth as a guide, one that encoded all you needed to know about landmarks, dangers, and sources of supply, and that helped you remember the vital information by putting into an engrossing story.

Let us recall that these uses of story are far from obsolete today. Not only do people still plan trips around sites important to a beloved novel, they also plan their lives with the help of stories. Perhaps you yourself decided you wanted to become a physician, teacher, artisan, or something else in part because of a movie you saw, or novel you read, in which such a figure was powerfully portrayed. Or how much you have learned about how to be a child, a student, later a mother or father, from exemplary models (or, if the experience was not good, from negative images) met on page or stage or screen. Of course we have had real-life models as well, but many are the persons who will acknowledge the influence of a fictional – mythic, if you wish – prototype of what she or he wants to be like. Moreover, like it or not, we often still find that a short story-like vignette or anecdote, even a topical cartoon, can help us to get a perspective on a current issue better than pages of abstract words.

Of course these stories were eventually written down. Such bards as Homer and Hesiod among the Greeks, or the bureaucrats of the imperial commissions assigned to record the Japanese accounts of "the age of the gods" from which the narrative above of Izanagi and Izanami comes, put them in writing once writing was invented and had moved beyond its first uses in commerce and magic. As one would expect of oral accounts, before being transcribed myths have many variants.

(The Japanese creation accounts appeared in two books: the *Kojiki*, of 712 C.E., the first Japanese book; and the much longer *Nihonshoki* of 720 C.E. Remarkably, the *Nihonshoki* records a number of their oral variants, almost like a modern folklore scholar, recognizing there is no one right version of a myth. After providing the "main" version, that text may add, "But one old man said. . ." or "In such-and-such a village they say. . ."[3])

MYTH RAW AND COOKED

The anthropologist Claude Lévi-Strauss, in a book called *The Raw and the Cooked*, declared that a myth is composed of all its variants, across both space and time.[4] Thus presumably the modern interpretation of a myth, or a modern story based on it, is just as much "the" myth as its ancient precedents. This is a view which will be important to the perspective of this book, because it seems to me to bring out what is lastingly true and important about myths in human experience. It is important to realize they, or their prototypes, had their origins in oral culture before writing; but a good myth did not stop there. Myths are stories told over and over, in many ways, and then provide themes woven into new myths, including those of stage and screen: that is all part of the process.

A novel like Charles Frazier's *Cold Mountain*, about a Confederate Civil War veteran making his long way home to North Carolina after the end of that fratricidal conflict, or James Joyce's famous (or infamous) *Ulysses*, both contain many episodes clearly based on Odysseus' protracted return to Ithaca after the Trojan War. Certain modern cinematic blockbusters were based directly on myths like *Beowulf*, or like *Star Trek*, *Star Wars*, or *The Lord of the Rings*, drew broadly from widespread mythic themes to create new epics set in the future or in alternative worlds, but in the mythic mode. To these dramatic films "fans" have responded as fervently as hearers circled around bards of yore. Now some of them wear costumes, form clubs, and profess to take the stories' mythic values very seriously, even seeing the heroic quests of Luke or Frodo as models for their own lives.

(The word "fan" is short for "fanatic," which in turn derives from the Latin *fanatici*, meaning devotees around the *fanum* or temple of a great deity.)

An understanding of myth, then, ought not only emphasize the original preliterate, oral-tradition versions as the "real" myth, implicitly regarding later written sources second-best.

To be sure, there are uses for this kind of analysis in some branches of scholarship. Moreover, it is always important to recall that these are stories with roots in human life as far back as it can be called human. The first myths were undoubtedly the first spoken human attempts to talk about the great questions of life: Where did we and the rest of the cosmos around us come from? How are we supposed to live our lives? How should we organize our society? What powers lurk out there that can affect us, and how do we deal with them?

These all-important issues were first handled through story (together with, of course, dance, ritual, and art, which probably were closely related to the story) and these stories reveal to us the creative imagination, the visions, the fears, and the sometimes fumbling responses of our ultimate human ancestors to this vast and baffling universe of which we find ourselves a tiny fragment.

Those first humans still dwell deep within us, both alien and familiar, and their dreads and dreams can still shape our own consciousnesses. The earliest fragments we still have of oral tradition, and transcripts from the telling of myths in cultures still oral at the time of European contact, such as most African, Pacific, and Native American societies, still hold that pristine power. They tell us: This is how people talked about the big questions when they had nothing to go by but their own dreams, imagination, experience, and words.

However, such myths do not die because culture changes. They live but change, in medium and sometimes in language, as the world moves on. To understand the overall and continuing impact of myth on human self-understanding, we need to take into account also the later literary versions that have appeared in the major literate cultures, like Homer's Iliad and Odyssey, the Bible, the Kojiki in Japan, or the Mahabharata, containing the Bhagavad-Gita (to be mentioned later) in India. In this form, the myth reaches far more people over many centuries than before, yet still continues to influence how people think about themselves, their values, and their society.

For though names may change, and spoken words become letters or even cinematic images, the myth lives on, for the basics of myth seem to be truly universally human, across time as well as space. Readers and scholars of myth alike are often impressed by how frequently similar motifs crop up far and wide. Creation out of a cosmic egg, for example, can be found from China and India to Greece and Native America. A divine voice calling for light over the face of dark cosmic waters can be found in both the Bible and Polynesia. Conflict between parents and children, or brother and brother, is very general. Some nineteenth-century scholars tried to make a case for diffusion, or the spread of myth from one culture to another. Undoubtedly this happens, but so widespread are many themes, in cultures that anciently could have had little contact, that one must look elsewhere for an explanation. Psychologists like Sigmund Freud and Carl G. Jung saw it instead in common human experiences, in childhood or simply embedded in the human psyche. We will look at these and other theories later.

Of course the literate versions of myth will, as myth should, connect past with present in fresh ways. In the Bible, the New Testament keeps in mind the earlier Hebrew Scriptures. One account of Ireland's foundation penned by medieval monks, although undoubtedly based on pre-Christian legends, has the Emerald Isle first settled by a son of Noah, who though denied a berth on the Ark built his own boat anyway and made his way to Ireland. When the flood came, a companion of his, Fintan, survived by changing himself successively into a salmon, an eagle, and a hawk; he lived 5,500 years, gaining vast wisdom and advising later arrivers about names and lore.[5]

Likewise, the founding of Rome, as recounted by the great poet Virgil in the Aeneid, was by the house of Aeneas, a prince of Troy who fled its destruction; the narrative is thus linked to the Iliad, Homer's classic epic of the Trojan War which was basic to education in the Roman world. All this is characteristic of national myths, which we will examine in more detail in a later chapter. They give their people distinguished origins, if only through linkages to other sources such as the Bible and the Iliad. National myths are also likely to give a nation's founders virtues, whether mystic wisdom like the Irish or brave endurance like the Roman, that its people like to think distinguishes their country, and may well indicate a special divine blessing on that folk.

Though based on traditional stories, for later readers, including us today, the "cooked" literary version of a myth probably has more power to do for *us*, later readers, what myth *does*, impart a world-view and model of life in story form, than would the rough snatches, fragments, and variants of oral tradition that were probably its raw material. Looking at a myth from the perspective of its total telling and impact down through the centuries, perceiving it as among those stories that tell us who we are, in this book we will often give primary importance to classic literary tellings.

A myth is not just any traditional story. It has to have a special significance for tellers and hearers. Some scholars, like Bronislaw Malinowski, have claimed a myth is properly about gods; those about heroes, he said, are legends, and those about ordinary people or animals are folktales. However, these distinctions may be too exacting. What does one do about the heroes of Greek myth, who often were half-divine and half-human? Or of Chinese myth, for in China many gods were once human, elevated by their heroism to heavenly status? Or stories which, while about human heroes and other first people who set patterns for society, otherwise functioned as its basic myths?

UNPACKING MYTH

The special significance of a myth lies in the way such a traditional story represents in narrative form the basic worldview of a society, as we saw in regard to those primal oral tellings and retellings. It encodes in story the fundamental principles: its social organization and way of life; its essential rituals, taboos, and other institutions; its dreams and its fears. We need to remember always that a myth is not just a story; it is also architecture, music, ritual, art, people's names, the organization of society. More than "ordinary" stories, however good or profound, real myth sets up a whole network of associations that may deeply dye many areas of one's life.

In the process, myth probably tells, as it recounts the various stages of creation, from the origin of the world to that of particular mountains or rivers, where it all came from. For we humans tend to think that if we know where something came from, what its origin was, we know what is really important about it: its true nature, its proper use, and what it says about the wider world. On that basis we build buildings and name babies.

Thus important myths are *etiological*, whatever else they may be; that is, they tell about origins. The myth earlier presented tells of the origin of the Japanese islands (nothing is said about the rest of the world in the Kojiki) as well as of numerous *kami* (gods) and lands, and also of death. Moreover, they implicitly give divine origin to key values and ways of understanding the universe and society. By remembering that the Japanese gods and islands were made through sexual encounters, this myth says that sex has its proper place at the very basis of the world as we know it, and that despite appearances the world is fundamentally biological, that is, *it is alive*. This reality is important for understanding and dealing with the forces around us. The perspective that life and consciousness run through and behind the universe is, one way or another, on many levels of sophistication, important to much of religion. For it says that our human nature, our aliveness, is not a freak in the galaxy, but is continuous with how the universe itself works, and has always worked from its onset.

The Izanagi/Izanami myth also establishes social institutions. The taboo on a woman speaking to a man before he had spoken to her, at least in a courtship situation, was very widespread not only in Japan but in much of the world until quite recently; relics of it remained even into the middle of the twentieth century, in that a boy could ask a girl for a "date," but the other way around was considered highly improper.

Teaching basic perspectives of the society, the Japanese myth presented a three-decker cosmos: heaven, earth, the dismal underworld of the dead. It established the principle that death and the realm of the dead are highly polluting. This is still the case in the traditional Japanese Shinto religion; funerals in Japan may be conducted in Buddhist temples, but not Shinto shrines. The story also shows that gods can come and go between heaven and earth freely; their descent is associated with difficult but creative ventures here below.

THE SHINING MAIDEN AND THE STORM GOD

Myths tend for form "cycles." The story goes on, and on and on. Amaterasu, emergent from Izanagi's left eye, went up to heaven where she established, in something like a heavenly model of the earthly, broad and narrow rice-fields, and a hall where she and her attendant maidens did weaving.

It was, at first, an idyllic scene. However, Amaterasu's brother, Susanoo, disliking his own assignment to earth while his sister and brother rode the sky, insisted he wished to follow his mother to the underworld. First, however, he determined to visit Amaterasu to bid her farewell. But as he stormily made his way upward to the sky, his sister, knowing full well his violent temper, dressed herself in warlike armor.

When the storm-god appeared, the sun-goddess challenged his motives, then suggested he prove himself by engaging with her in a friendly contest of procreation, seeing who could produce the most offspring by magical means. But they quarreled over the results, and Susanoo's rage quickly went out of control. He rampaged through his sister's heavenly rice-fields, stamping on the plants and ruining the irrigation ditches. He defecated in a room where the harvest festival was celebrated each fall, defiling it. Finally, he polluted the heavenly weaving-hall, hurling across its purified floor the backward-flayed body of a pony. Amaterasu, outraged and terrified beyond measure, retreated into the rock-cave of heaven, depriving the earth of light.

By now all the gods were concerned about what is going on. They gathered in the River of Heaven (the Milky Way) to discuss the matter. Finally, a goddess named Ama-no-Uzume arose and, standing on an upturned tub, began a ribald dance, causing the assembled deities to break out in peals of raucous laughter. In the meantime, a sacred evergreen tree had been placed near the entrance of the cave, a sacred mirror hung from it, and a strong god concealed himself nearby.

Before long the hidden goddess became curious as to what was going on outside her dim cave to cause such merriment. She stuck her head out, and immediately was fascinated by her own beauty as reflected in the mirror. She proceeded further and further out. The god at the door took her by the hand, and a sacred rope, the *shimenawa*, was placed across the entrance of the cave to prevent her re-entry. Light, day, and loveliness had returned to the world.

As for Susanoo, the gods exiled him to earth. However, there his nature seemed to change, for it is well known that the *kami* possess both a "rough" and "smooth" nature, a wild, warlike character, and a gentle, pacific side. Amaterasu herself showed both natures by appearing as an armored warrior, then as a mild maiden distressed at tumult and desecration. Now, below the clouds, the storm god redeemed himself by rescuing a young woman from a dragon and, marrying her, establishing the land of Izumo in western Japan.[6] (In the same way, the typhoons of Japan can rage all night; then, the next day, a peculiar calm, limpid air hangs amid the devastation.)

MYTH AND MEANING

By now we may be asking ourselves more and more insistently what this seemingly bizarre story *means*? Why was it repeatedly recited in ancient, preliterate Japan, finally making its way into the nation's first book?

Obviously the narrative possessed an enchantment of some kind to cause it to be told over and over. Perhaps it was just a good story: colorful, even if a little gross in its humor. Yet like any really good story, it contained images a hearer might recognize, and customs she would comprehend. The mirror, evergreen, and rope would look familiar to anyone who had seen them at a shrine of the *kami*. The behavior of Izanami and Amaterasu in this tale would bespeak the paradoxical combination of strength and submissiveness of many Japanese women. The myth was not an allegory, with a one-to-one symbolic meaning making it a kind of code which, deciphered, tells us something quite different from its surface connotation. (Some people read the Bible this way.) It was in plain, not code. Yet at the same time the narration seemed both meaningful, and the kind of tale that just keeps one wondering what will happen next.

The point is, a myth is a story. That the world of beginnings is told in story form is a starting-point, for our *lives* are stories, not just abstractions or allegories of something else. We need, therefore, a larger story of the universe into which our own petite story can be slipped. This larger, mythic story should be *polyvalent*, meaning and telling several things at once; it may simultaneously relate of the origin and nature of the universe, the character of the gods, the commencement of rituals and customs, and the fundamental energies and creative tensions that keep it going.

On the last point, as mentioned the old Japanese myths make clear that the universe is alive and biological as well as material, at least in its first phase: the two gods create it sexually rather than by fiat, as a single deity might have. We find their myth-universe, like our own lives, riven by deepseated polarities: purity and pollution, heaven and earth, male and female, calm and tempestuous temperament, life and death. Out of the energies generated by friction between opposites things happen; the formation of the world and the struggles of human society.

A creation myth like this, then, is not just a prescientific presentation of how the world came into being, intended only to answer a scientific kind of curiosity. It is rather a story of creation that at one and the same time makes human life and society absolutely continuous with that creation, and the whole cosmos. It shows how our problems and possibilities were built into the stuff of the universe itself. The universe is made humanly significant, and the gods who made our portion of it are part of a larger, ongoing framework. In passing, we might recollect that, while we would not accept these myths as literal history or science, the matter of making the universe humanly significant (the term is Peter Berger's[7]) remains a fundamental issue, grappled with in many ways by science, philosophy, literature, and religion – and is a major theme of what we will call "modern myth."

Furthermore, the Amaterasu/Susanoo continuation gives us additional insights into Japanese society. Here we see the principal woman in another role than Izanami's. Even though Amaterasu demurely retreats into the cave, she exercises real power from within it – just as Japanese women even today, though theoretically subordinate, often manifest substantial power through home and family.

Then consider the assembly of the gods in the River of Heaven talking it out until they decide what to do. This is a very Japanese way of going about it. Whether in family, business, or government, the real decisions are not necessarily made by those who outwardly appear to have positions of power, but by councils that go on and on until there is a sense that a consensus has been reached; then the apparent authority-figure may at least be the one to announce it.

Finally, the mirror, sacred evergreen, and *shimenawa* are still features of every Shinto shrine. Like the goddess's, fertility dances performed at Shinto festivals have been quite uninhibited in the past. In many ways, this story is a sort of charter for much in Japanese, especially Shinto, society. Myths explain, instruct, justify, warn. But other considerations present themselves. What kind of world do the myths inhabit, and who are these beings, called gods though they often seem quite human, who dwell therein?

Mythic action gives the impression of having taken place long ago, in a time so far back in time and so near the beginning that one cannot speak of it in terms of dates, or years since then, It was a different *kind* of time. The world was not fixed in its final form. Magic and miracles could still happen, and the beings of that era were often gods and heroes, and their like acted far more freely in the world then than now.

Those gods seem to be both nature and individual personalities. Amaterasu is both "sky-shiner," light of the sky, and a personality capable of getting angry, feisty, maybe depressed. So also is Susanoo at once the storm and a stormy personality. Indeed, if anything describes gods and heroes in myth, it is ability, and willingness, to take human feelings and appetites to an extreme, superhuman degree: their rages, their loves, their indulgences in food, drink, and sex are off the charts compared to the ordinary human.

The gods are immortal, if we count Izanami as not really dying but transferring to Yomi, where she reigns forever as a kind of queen of the dead. They can make mistakes through impetuosity, and all that they do, good or bad, especially in this time of beginnings, has a continuing effect on the cosmos and human life down to this day. The gods may know a great deal, but they are not omniscient or all-knowing; the primal couple needed to consult a higher god, who in turn had to use some form of divination, to discover what their sin was. They have superhuman powers – being able to descend and ascend between heaven and earth – but are not omnipotent or all-powerful, since Izanami could suffer from burns.

All this may make us feel that myths are simply weird, irrelevant to life in the modern world. Yet somehow we want to keep hearing them. They may seem like children's stories, but of course the child is still somewhere inside us. We may find myths both off-putting and unforgettable, like something from one's own distant past.

The eminent historian of religion Mircea Eliade concluded that all real myths were fundamentally creation myths, like the Japanese examples we have already presented; they were tales of origin, set in the sacred time of the beginning. Knowing origins is extremely important in archaic societies, because that establishes and legitimates the way a thing is done now. Asked why a certain ritual is performed, or moral taboo observed, people for whom myths are living will say, "Because that is the way the ancestors did it at the beginning." Often a healing ritual will not work, or a religious observance seem properly performed, unless the myth of its origin in mythic time is recited as part of its performance.

The creation myth tells how the world and humanity first came into being, and not seldom has a coda explaining how, a little later, evil and death came into the world, though the cosmos may originally have been made perfect by God or the gods. But though humanity and heaven were once in close rapport one with the other, something went wrong to disrupt this relationship, like the burning of Izanami or the fall of Adam and Eve in the Garden of Eden. Then a further kind of myth is called for, almost like a corrective to creation and "fall," and one that also has resonance down to the present.

HERO MYTH

Let us take another story. In a galaxy long ago and far away there dwells a young man. He is living with an uncle, on whose farm he has to work even though he dreams of going to the space academy, and his real father is not much talked of. Then, one day, while looking for a strayed robot, he encounters a strange old man, who seems to know quite a bit about his father, whom he says was killed by dark forces. The elder gives the young visitor a valuable weapon, a light saber, that had belonged to his father.

Not long after, the dark forces destroy the aunt and uncle. The youth is now ready to join the older mentor on a great quest to rescue a princess and save the galaxy from evil usurpers of power. During the course of their journey he visits a hangout of desperate characters (where he and his guide find a pilot), acquires a small band of helpers; visits and ultimately destroys a "Death Star" (a gigantic maze-like base of the enemy); and is sent to an eminent teacher in the use of the Force, the inner spiritual power of the universe.

Yet in at least two instances the youthful warrior seems to possess a higher wisdom than his two older instructors. Out of compassion he leaves to help his friends in danger when the elders insist he must first complete his training. And when he learns that the Prince of the Dark Side is actually his father, "dead" to his former self and now given over to evil, he rejects the advice that he must simply kill him. He is aware through a kind of deep empathy that his twisted parent still has some good in him. He is in the end reconciled to his father and saves him, even as the dark lord and his empire die, and justice is restored.

This is of course the story of Luke Skywalker in the cinematic epic *Star Wars*, the original trilogy screened 1977–83. It is like a modern example of the hero myth. For while a hero may have lived near the time of the creation and wrought his marvelous deeds in the mythic time of the beginning, that is not necessarily the case. Some figures around whom many of the attributes of the hero myth gathered lived later, perhaps in their own sort of mythical time, perhaps instead in historical time as we know it. But they had a very special role in relation to the mythic time of the beginning, or of a more ideal past, just as the heroes of *Star Wars* were called to restore the better galaxy of before the Empire.

The hero in some such myths is one who, in this situation of estrangement from paradise, finds a way back to the original good, or something approaching it, and is able to lead others there. Religious leaders in this role, also called saviors, like Moses, Jesus, the Buddha, or Krishna, may in a real sense return to the primal right relationship. Those who are more figures from the world of action, the warrior-hero like Beowulf, Hercules, David, Rama, or Luke Skywalker, or King Arthur's Knights of the Holy Grail contending with the Wasteland, may simply restore a righteous kingdom, but their deeds have overtones of world-redemption nonetheless, and their epics count among the great myths.

Hero-myths, like *Star Wars*, have attracted tremendous followings in the twentieth and twenty-first centuries in both book and screen versions, as did stories of King Arthur and Camelot, or Germanic heroes, like Siegfried as portrayed in the operas of Richard Wagner, in the nineteenth century. Other twentieth-century examples would certainly include the books and films of L. Frank Baum's *The Wizard of Oz*, J. R. R. Tolkien's *The Lord of the Rings*, *Titanic* (with the heroine, Rose, descending into the depths of the sinking ship to rescue her love), and the *Star Trek* TV series and movies. It is, moreover, well known that *Star Wars* was based on features of the hero myth categorized by the mythologist Joseph Campbell in his classic work, *The Hero with a Thousand Faces* (1949).

As the title suggests, Campbell believed that all hero myths were really just one myth, what he called the "monomyth," and that finally these myths were not stories of figures "back then," but were about ourselves, here and now. The hero offers a template or model of a human life – the problems one must confront, the initiations one must undergo, the achievements one must realize, to be truly successful. Some of the titles of stages into which Campbell divided the "monomyth" in his analysis are suggestive of this role, as they are of Luke in *Star Wars*: "The Call to Adventure," "The Road of Trials," "The Meeting with the Goddess," "Atonement with the Father," "The Ultimate Boon," "Master of Two Worlds," and finally "Freedom to Live," among others.

Campbell's approach was not well regarded by many conventional scholars of myth. He was accused of being highly selective as he extracted mythic episodes that fit his thesis from all sorts of cultures, without regard for the complete story or its original cultural context, as well as of using later literary versions of myths rather than the original in all its variants. Critics have also pointed out that not all ancient heroes have fitted his idealizing picture.

All these arguments with Campbell are certainly true. Yet some accounting must also be made of the remarkable impact his work, and others like it, has had in our own time. Whether or not Campbell presented his myths with scholarly accuracy, he presented them, in books, in lectures, on television, in a way that seemed to connect with the deep spiritual yearnings of many modern people. One might almost say he created a "myth of myth," a narrative based on his "monomyth" suggesting that salvation could be found in rightly appropriating ancient myths, because they could tell us how to find story, meaning, and "Freedom to Live" in our own very modern lives. This was what Campbell clearly most wanted to do; as one critic said, he was oddly not really concerned about myth – as myth – but with mythology as a vehicle for delivering inner, psychological liberation to his contemporary audiences, and like most preachers he was far more concerned with saving the world than with footnotes.[8]

What Campbell's work, and the also popular twentieth-century writing on myth of Carl Jung and Mircea Eliade, tell us most emphatically that in the kind of story usually labeled myth, above all the hero myth, something lives to which moderns respond as much as anyone. Not all moderns. Critics have rightly pointed to dangers inherent in what might be called "mythic thinking," with its tendency to oversimplify good and evil into "good guys" and "bad guys," the children of light against the minions of darkness; to suggest that problems can have magical, prescientific solutions; and to exalt heroes who use violence all too freely. Such tainted myths about race, revolution, and history lay behind fascism, communism, and many other contemporary evils.

Yet most of those who read, and who flocked to see on the silver screen *The Wizard of Oz*, *Star Wars*, *The Lord of the Rings*, and *Star Trek*, do not seem to have been seduced into the Dark Side of the Force. They saw instead a sort of innocent idealism in the heroes and their companions, and most profoundly perhaps something that could be held up against the problems, needs, and deepest dreams of their own lives. They also felt the fascination of an alternative world, full of wonder and joy.

Some might question whether these recent books and films can properly be called myth, if by that term one means a traditional story with roots in preliterate society. Perhaps so, and if one prefer to call these works "stories of the mythic type" instead of "modern myths," fine. But to my mind too restrictive a definition does not adequately facilitate a full appreciation of what, for better or worse, such tales, clearly in the mold of ancient myth, have meant in all sorts of human settings, conveyed in many media, both then and now.

For while Joseph Campbell may oversimplify the matter, it is beyond doubt that something is there that cries out for understanding. It is related to the way our own lives are not abstractions, scientific or philosophical, but stories. This understanding will be a basic theme of this book.

CHAPTER 2

THE ELF-KING'S CAVE: TYPES OF MYTH

In the Wide World the Wood-elves lingered in the twilight of our Sun and Moon, but loved best the stars; and they wandered in the great forests that grew tall in lands that are now lost . . . In a great cave some miles within the edge of Mirkwood on its eastern side there lived at this time their greatest king. Before his huge doors of stone a river ran out of the heights of the forest and flowed on and out into the marshes at the feet of the high wooded lands. This great cave, from which countless smaller ones opened out on every side, wound far underground and had many passages and wide halls . . .

J. R. R. Tolkien, *The Hobbit*[1]

The world of myth is that cave, with many rooms and hidden connections. In this chapter we will name and epitomize the major chambers.

CREATION MYTHS

We have noted that Mircea Eliade considered all myths to be creation myths, in the sense that they establish the origin of something in mythic time, and thereby give it a special and irrevocable charter. No doubt there is a sense in which this is true. However, the relation of particular myths to the original creation can be quite varied, and it is here that categorization becomes quite interesting. We will now review briefly several types, then deal with each more fully in subsequent chapters of this book.

The story may be of the original creation directly – or at least what is given of it – like the Japanese Izanami/Izanagi account given above. In one Australian Aboriginal story, from the Arrente people, the earth was first just an empty plain. All was dark; neither life nor death was real. The sun, moon, and stars, together with the ancestors, slept beneath the earth.

But finally the primal ones awoke, or at least moved from deep sleep without dreams to dreaming, for they arose into what is called the Dreamtime. In this timeless state, they wandered the land, sometimes in animal form: as the kangaroo, or lizard, or bird, or as part human and part animal or plant. They sang, and their pathways are now called songlines; one can follow them, and mystically enter Dreamtime and join in their timeless labors, by singing their songs and following where they lead.

Two of these eternal ones discovered half-made human beings, with constituent materials, but like balls or bundles, shapeless and unfinished. Made out of animals or plants, these formless humans were found near water holes or lakes. The wandering creators, called the Ungambikula, took stone knives and carved people, with faces and hands and everything, out of the raw material. But each man or women owed enduring loyalty to the animal or plant – lizard, grub, parakeet, grass, tree – out of which she or had been made; that was the individual's, and the tribe's, totem.

After this labor, the creating ancestors went back to sleep, back to the Dreamtime, either underground or as rocks and trees. But they left marks of their presence in the form of sacred rocks or trees or wells, and by following the trail made by these signs, often enhanced by rock paintings, one can follow the path to the Dreamtime. For that sacred time of origins is an ever-present reality, set invisibly over against this world, from which we all come and to which we will return between this present life and the next; we can now return to it in dreams and in the dance of festivals. This is clearly an account which explains much in Aboriginal life: not only the totem, but also the dancing, the thought about the universe, the deep psychology.[2]

Many creation myths begin with chaos in the form of water or an endless sea, and with a cosmic egg; natural, since in common observation life emerges out of moisture and out of eggs. A Chinese creation myth first posits primordial chaos as a cloud of mist in the shape of an egg. Within it, the first man, Pan Gu, took shape and, in the heart of the egg, awoke to life. Like an infant in the womb he thrashed around, breaking the eggshell and scattering its substance, the stuff of life, in all directions. The purer *yang* elements rose upwards to become heaven, the denser *yin* aspects to earth.[3] (In the traditional Chinese *yang/yin* symbolism, *yang* is masculine, sky, sun, day, heights, the first half of the year of lengthening days and seed-time; *yin* is female, earth, moon, night, valleys, the last half of the year, of shortening days and harvest, among other more esoteric qualities. In principle both are equally good and bad, and what is essential is balance, though in practice *yang* is often favored.)

THE NEXT GENERATION

Next, in an "in the beginning" story come the gods and heroes of what might be called the "next generation." The primal moments have passed, but we are still in the mythic divine age, not in time as we know it. An example is the Egyptian myth of Isis and Osiris. This brother and sister pair, also husband and wife (like the pharaoh, who customarily married his sister), were great-grandchildren of Re, or Atum-Re, the mighty sun-god, creator, and ruler of the world from his high vantage point in the sky. Osiris, bursting with life, vitality, and good-will, was a god of fertility and giver of culture to humankind. But his older brother Seth, who embodied disorder and destruction, was wildly jealous of Osiris's popularity. The elder brother killed the younger and, not content with murder, according to one version cut his body into pieces and scattered them across the land.

Osiris's sister-wife Isis, mistress of magic, was distraught. In her grief she searched and searched until she had found all the pieces of her mate, put them back together, and by her mystic arts ani-mated the reassembled corpse just long enough for him to impreg-nate her with a son, Horus. Then Osiris departed to reign over the beautiful western Kingdom of the Dead. The story goes on to describe a protracted conflict between Horus and Seth, with many gods including Isis, and Osiris from the Other World, intervening. As both humans and gods will, in the heat of battle both displayed faults stemming from out-of-control anger. But Horus, represent-ing order, finally prevailed to become ruler of Egypt personified by the pharaoh. Seth retired to his eternal realm of storm and desola-tion, perhaps suggested by the desert wastes around the Valley of the Nile.[4]

This cycle of myths demonstrates well what the demigods of the "next generation" usually do: build the link between the primal creation and the ordering of human society. That all-important transition is not without struggle, but order eventually is established. Yet this cycle is also placed back in mythic time, when the world is still in flux and magic is potent. In our different, later age, the link to the times of the Beginning is fragile, needing to be maintained carefully by kings, priests, and heroes.

The famous Nordic gods of Valhalla, including Odin, Thor, and the trickster Loki, are from this second generation. At first there was only ice and fire: simplifying the story a little, from melting ice emerged Odin and his brothers, and they created the world, its people, and other gods from the body of Ymir, an immense giant. It was Odin who hung on the world-tree nine days and lost an eye to obtain wisdom, and Thor who fought monsters, even as Loki delighted in impeding his fellow deities with his clever deceptions; here are the makings of many a plot.[5]

HERO MYTHS

Other myths, especially the later hero myths of the kind associated with Joseph Campbell, or modern cinematic epics, occurred perhaps much later, but still present hints of a better primal world that the hero sets out to restore, however partially and imperfectly. We shall consider heroes to be of two types: the warrior hero (who in turn are, in our terms, the champion and the quester), and the savior.

Warrior hero stories may begin with the protagonist confronting a monster or demon who gets in the way of the world's being as good as it ought to be: the Greek Theseus destroying the Minotaur of Crete; St George battling the dragon; Beowulf, the hero of the oldest English poem, slaying Grendel; or Rama, in India, rescuing his abducted wife Sita from the demon Ravana. No less in the warrior-hero lineage are many more recent stalwarts of "westerns," like the Lone Ranger, or Flash Gordon of comic strip and screen.

The savior hero's myth career may outwardly follow the same pattern as that of the warrior – special birth or upbringing, trials, initiation, ultimate victory and rulership – but is on a different plane. For his victories are not those of the sword so much as of the spirit, and the resultant kingdom is inward but everlasting. We are thinking, of course, of figures like Krishna, the Buddha, Laozi, Jesus, Muhammad; we will examine their stories later.

IN MY END IS MY BEGINNING

Myths of *eschatology* are of the last times: stories like those of the Christian Last Judgment, the coming of the Future Buddha, Maitreya, or the Nordic Ragnorak, the "Twilight of the Gods."

(Note that though Ragnorak was a tragic defeat for the gods of Valhalla, hope remained that the earth would be renewed again, fresh and pristine, under the benign god Balder. Often the consummation of one world is, as in Hindu, Buddhist, and Greek eschatology, part of a greater cycle of creation and destruction, over and over, or as in Zoroastrian, Jewish and Christian eschatology only prepares the way for the creation of a new heaven and earth.)

The end of the world is inevitably related to its beginning, since we find that religious or mythic views of the end of the world inevitably have a close symmetry with creation: either they are an incoming of a "Kingdom of God" that restores the primal paradise, or prelude to a new creation or cycle in which the process starts over again.

In some religions the process is irreversible. The Zoroastrian vision in ancient Persia, which undoubtedly had some influence on the eschatology of later Judaism, and of Christianity and Islam, declared that this world now is the scene of a great battle between good and evil. The hosts of Ahura Mazda, the Lord of Light, are ranged against his rival, Angra Mainyu, and his demons of darkness. But at the appointed time a savior, Saoshyant, will appear to effect the final defeat of evil, restoring creation to its original perfection. Hell will be emptied, its denizens now turned to righteousness, and the demons with their leader killed. All humankind will be given a wonderful drink of immortality, the world becoming as endlessly beautiful and benign as its maker had intended at the outset. But now goodness is everlasting; the first "fall" will not come a second time.[6]

INDIVIDUAL JOURNEYS BEYOND THE WORLD

What about the afterlife career of the individual? What happens to one after she or he dies? Perhaps the doctrinal answer to this inevitable human query is not strictly myth, but that concept is closely connected to the society's myths, for it will make sense only in the context of the overall view of heaven, earth, and underworld, together with the origin and meaning of human life, presented in those myths. The individual's afterlife is like an individualized part of the mythic cosmological and eschatological scenarios.

In the case of Zoroastrianism, for example, after a three-day waiting period, the soul of the deceased is taken into the presence of mighty angelic judges of the dead, who weigh the soul. If good is greater than evil, the entrant into the divine world perceives a beautiful maiden, who represents a good conscience. But if judgment goes the other way, he beholds the ugly face worn by a twisted mind instead.

Nonetheless, all spirits then proceed to the Chinvat Bridge, leading to heaven across the abyss of hell. For the righteous, it is a broad highway on which the blessed enter joyously into realms of light, but for the wicked it become narrow as a razor, and they fall down into the dismal underworld below. However, as we have seen, at the end of the world-drama, Ahura Mazda empties both heaven and hell; the wicked are purged of their sin; and all live together eternally in a paradisal new earth.

Here we see clearly personal application of the mythic cosmology: this world is the scene of a mighty war between Ahura Mazda and Angra Mainyu, in which individual choice is crucial, and one must accept the consequences of one's choice. Although it is by no means apparent now, Ahura Mazda, the Lord of Light, will win the war in the end; this is a once-for-all victory, and time moves one-way toward that consummation.[7]

Reminiscent of these realms of light, and perhaps influenced by Zoroastrianism, is the form of Buddhism known as Pure Land, very widespread and influential in East Asia. It tells that ages ago, a buddha attained enlightenment who came to be known as Amitabha, or Amida in Japanese. Out of compassion for all beings, he vowed that all who called upon his name in faith would be brought into his Pure Land after death. A "Pure Land" is like an aura – extending perhaps for billions of miles – surrounding a great enlightened being, generated by the power and purity of his profound meditations. For lesser individuals who are brought into such an aura it comes into focus as endless lands of incomparable beauty: trees filled with networks of jewels, perfumed rivers, heavenly music on the air.[8]

This vision of Amida's Pure Land wherein the faithful are reborn clearly puts into narrative form several Buddhist themes: the power of meditation to create thought which, in its pure form, as one's own "buddha-nature" within, is infinite, all-powerful, and all-compassionate; the Mahayana Buddhist teaching there are count-less buddhas and countless worlds throughout the endless seas of space and time; the importance of "taking refuge" in the Buddha, and of negating one's own ego – which Pure Land teachers say is the deeper meaning of relying on the strength of another, Amida, rather than oneself. It restores an original right relationship of the individ-ual to deep-level reality; typically, in the Buddhist case, not prior in time, but present all the time, though apparent only to those whose perception is cleansed.

The traditional Christian teaching of gaining salvation into eternal life through faith in the power of Jesus Christ is clearly com-parable. It also fits neatly into a larger traditional scenario, in this case of God's creating the world, of the fall into sin or alienation from God of the primal parents, Adam and Eve; Christ's redemptive work as a savior/hero makes it possible for the original right rela-tionship between God and humanity to be restored through adher-ence to him, in this life and the life to come.

CHARTER MYTHS

Finally, we need to direct attention to three subcategories of myth which, while perhaps aspects of creation, the "next generation," the hero myth, or the eschatological myth, deserve special notice.

First are what might be called the local or specific etiological or "charter" myths, giving the mythic origin of a particular site, like a sacred mountain or river, or the location of a particular temple, or the rationale and ritual action of a particular rite. For the devout Muslim, for example, Mecca is not the sacred city only because it was the city of the Muhammad. Even before the days of the Prophet, its Ka'bah, or "Holy House," was a holy site, the supreme place for humankind to worship. It was said to have been built first by Adam, who placed in its walls the "Black Stone" that fell from heaven as a sign, and was rebuilt by Abraham and other of the lineage of great prophets down to the last, Muhammad. But this great shrine fell into idolatry, housing the worship of false deities of sun, moon, and stars, during the "Age of Ignorance." But just as the Prophet called human-ity back to the original pure monotheism, so he restored the Ka'bah to its original role as the center of that worship.[9]

The historian of religion Mircea Eliade, especially in *The Sacred and the Profane*, emphasized that religious sites are not just chosen casually, but are markers of such a "hierophany," or divine manifestation, making it a blessed place.[10] Examples can be multiplied, from the prodigious signs of fire, cloud, and sounding trumpets which showed Sinai to be the Mountain of God, to Joseph Smith's guidance to the right place to construct the temple of the Latter-Day Saints. Pilgrimage places are especially regarded as sites of hierophanies, like Mecca: whether those Roman Catholic shrines to modern apparitions of Our Lady like Lourdes and Fatima; or Hindu sites like Rameswaram in south India, associated with events in the great hero-epic the Ramayana; or Banaras, Hinduism's most holy city, sacred to Shiva, whose hierophany here is said to have taken the form of Shiva's *lingam* or sacred pillar bursting forth from the earth and piercing the sky, unending and overflowing with light; or Mount Kilauea in Hawaii, home and manifestation of the fire-goddess Pele.

Among the Yoruba of Nigeria, in Africa, it was said that their great city Ife ("Wide House") marks the site where Obatala, envoy or son of the high god Olorun, commenced creation of the earth. He had been lowered down on a golden chain to the expanse below, then nothing but water. Olorun had given him a bag containing only what he needed: a snail shell full of sand, a white hen, a black cat, and a palm nut.

When the chain was all let out and Obatala was hanging over the water, he began to panic; but Olorun called out to him, "The sand!" He sprinkled it on the water. Then he dropped the chicken, which scratched the sand, scattering it in all directions, where it formed dry land. Obatala then descended himself, planted the palm nut as the beginning of vegetation, and named the place where he decided to dwell Ife. He lived there for some days with only the cat as companion, but eventually made people out of clay to share his realm, and in this way Ife became the city of Ife, and Obatala became its ruler, establishing its kingly lineage.[11]

Many origin myths, of course, are not about such weighty matters. They may have to do with specific places, objects, or even constellations. Among the Iroquois it was told that the Pleiades were originally a group of seven children who would not stop dancing. In desperation, their parents stopped giving them food, but they just became lighter and lighter until they floated up into the sky and became the famous cluster. The Ila people of Zambia say that fire was brought down from heaven by the mason wasp, an insect which often builds its nests around fireplaces.

NATIONAL MYTHS

Because of their importance, not always benign, in world history down to the present, we need also to mention national and nationalistic myths, those purporting to explain the origin, character, and destiny of particular peoples. The Yoruba myth just cited is an example of this type as well (for myths are polyvalent); it tells also that the princes other than Obatala were required to bow before him, and though they were given small lands to rule, they had to acknowledge his supremacy. In Japan likewise, as we have seen, Amaterasu sent down her divine grandson to quell the tumultuous good and evil kami disturbing the peace of the lands below; his grandson in turn became Jimmu Tenno, the first emperor, supposedly proclaimed in 640 B.C.E. by the Western calendar.

In 1940, at the height of Japan's period of extreme nationalism and militarism, with Emperor Hirohito, said to be Jimmu's 124th successor on the chrysanthemum throne, the alleged 2,400th anniversary of this highly legendary event occurred. Much was then made of it, with a holiday, special Shinto processions and services, and a further tightening of governmental control in the name of the sacred sovereign.

In such ways as this, myths important to the distinctive self-definition of a people can be used to enhance a sense of nationalistic identity. The Tudor monarchs of England employed stories of King Arthur, from whom they claimed descent, to enhance their legitimacy, and King Arthur again became very popular in the Victorian and Edwardian eras, in conjunction with the ideology of empire, chivalry, and the gentleman.

MYTHS OF EVIL

Next, there are what may be called "myths of evil," treating of the origin and nature of evil in the world. While these narratives are broadly parts of the creation or subsequent stories, it is helpful to call them particularly to notice, since the way in which the contours of evil are viewed can offer significant insight into a culture.

Why is evil so embedded in the world, however much way we may wish it otherwise? Generally it is recognized that in some way evil is an anomaly, the "abomination of desolation" "standing where it ought not," in the words of the New Testament. It is something that ought not to be, yet is; an incongruous flaw is what otherwise might seem to be a rational universe; pointless yet so powerful. Explanations vary greatly.

In Zoroastrianism, as we have seen, good and evil are often represented as primordial twins, together from the beginning, but opposites and at war. In Christianity, though the same opposition stands between two cosmic forces, good and evil, God and Satan, they are generally not held to have been equal from the beginning. Satan, originally Lucifer, the "Light-bearer," was an angel who rebelled against his Lord over what he saw as the demeaning honor heaven was to give God's next creation, humanity. In his pride, Satan said, according to John Milton in *Paradise Lost*, he would rather reign in hell than serve in heaven.

In the same way, in these two monotheistic (or, in this respect, almost quasi-dualistic) religions, evil is the result of choices. To this day dualism demands a choice, for the two paired entities, God and Satan, continually try to draw us each to his side in the great war. We help God and the good win when we choose his cause, and aid Satan's side by aligning with him. As so often, the myth constructs a worldview that gives meaning to what an individual does. It probably no less constructs edifices within the believer's mind and heart. Not a few devout followers of such a God of choice have felt the eternal warfare deep within their consciousness, as well as in cosmos and history.

Yet other myths make evil seems more a matter of bad luck, or of innocent wrong choices. Sir James Frazer told the curious story of a tribe on Sulawesi (Celebes) in Indonesia who said that originally the sky where the creator dwelt was very near the earth, and he would lower gifts down on a rope to his children. Once he thus let down a stone, but the first men and women were indignant at such a useless gift and refused it. So the creator pulled it back up and lowered instead a banana. This they took. But the creator called to them, "Because you have chosen the banana, your life shall be like its life. Had you taken the stone, you would have been like it, changeless and immortal."[12]

In the more sophisticated Eastern religions, as we will see, ignorance is likewise the culprit rather than direct rebellion against God in full knowledge of the consequences. We choose evil because we cannot, or will not, see that the pleasures it offers end in suffering.

We do not fully comprehend how everything is transitory and passing away, including our own ego-self. (In the last analysis, perhaps the interpretations of evil as rebellion or as ignorance are not as far apart as might seem on the surface, for only a rather willful, determined, rebellious ignorance could fail to see its own consequences, and on the other hand rebellion could only be explained as the result of blind ignorance of the true nature of reality.

In Buddhist mythology, Mara, the lower god who tries to tempt or distract the Buddha from attaining enlightenment on the eve of that great achievement, really expresses both sides. He is not presented as wholly and utterly evil so much as what Joseph Campbell called a "holdfast" deity: one who just wants to keep things as they are. Mara was said to be one of the old Vedic gods of weather and nature, and a stickler for traditional ritual. But he was just perceptive enough to see that if a human being like the Buddha became enlightened, that master would be greater than his kind, and his days as supreme would be numbered. The Buddha would become "Teacher of Gods and Men," but Mara seemed sure the world-enlightened one could teach him nothing of importance. Hence his stubborn resistance: pride like Lucifer's in his status, including his rank above human beings; ignorance so great as to make him think he had nothing more to learn.

About myth, however, there is always something more to be learned. Take the many modern theories about myth . . .

CHAPTER 3

THE VIEW FROM OUTSIDE: THEORIES OF MYTH

TYPES OF THEORIES

Here are several leading theories of myth and meaning. After reviewing them, we will end this chapter with cautions about all such theories, even about the concept of myth itself. We are now, as it were, moving from myth to mythology.

At the outset, it is important to appreciate that *these* are theories for looking at myth from an exterior point of view – not taking them at face value, but asking, "Why did people tell stories like these?" "What were they really trying to say or do by means of such tales?" And, many would add, "What can they mean to us?" "Are they just absurd superstition we are better off without? Can they help us to understand ancient people? Can they help us to understand ourselves?" Answers, needless to say, range very widely, and that range is what we will try to grasp.

The theories are here divided into four types: Euhemeric, Enlightenment, Romantic, and Pedagogical. Examples of all four can be found in most periods, from antiquity on up: whenever someone looks at a myth, not just as a good story or as "what all of us around here believe," but from an analytic point of view, some kind of theory or outside framework for understanding is there. The four types seem to me to reflect not only perceptions in a formal sense, but also deep-seated attitudes or ways of thinking on the part of their proponents. Perhaps you will find yourself somewhere along the spectrum.

Of course much overlap may be found among these types; many theories, like many myths, like a faceted jewel, can be looked at from the perspective of two, three, or four angles. But the division into types may be of interest, though here we can only summarize the range of myth-theories. In the later chapter on mythologists we will examine some of the principal individual approaches in more detail.

EUHEMERIC THEORIES

The Greek writer Euhemeros (330–260 B.C.E.) claimed, like many rationalistic commentators since, that myths are not factually true.[1] They were based on historical events, but then much exaggerated in telling and retelling. The gods were really just great kings or other figures of stature who over many years were made into deities. Working as he did in the court of Alexander the Great, Euhemeros must have had ample opportunity to see the beginning of this process; Alexander was in time to become the virtually deified subject of miracle-filled epics throughout Asia.

Later, skeptical Roman authors like Lucretius used Euhemeros' approach to demystify myths that seemed incredible, as did medieval Christians seeking natural explanations of gods who, in the light of their faith, could not be taken as authentic objects of worship. Snorri Sturluson, in the "Prose Edda," demoted his old Norse gods into ancient heroes. The spirit of Euhemeros seems to live on in many modern biblical scholars engaged in "The Quest of the Historical Jesus," in the title of Albert Schweitzer's landmark book, or in quest of the historical Moses. Euhemeros has no less influenced other modern researchers, Eastern and Western, as they cast a critical gaze at such figures as the Buddha, Krishna, or Laozi, seeking to strip away encrustations of myth and miracle, and discover the impressive but quite human individual underneath it all.

Euhemeric interpretations of myth – very common today whether the name is used or not – tend to make myth only an early form of something else. It is "primitive" science or philosophy, or "misremembered" history, told today with a smile that says, "now we know better." The Euhemeric spirit has been accused of reductionism, that is, of saying myth is "nothing but" something primitive and credulous. It does not, critics say, appreciate the other facets of psychological or spiritual meaning present in a story like that of Isis or Amaterasu. But few commentators on myth have been untouched by Euhemerism as they try to wrestle with stories that seem important yet cannot be literally true in a modern scientific sense.

ENLIGHTENMENT THEORIES

By this category we mean views of myth that essentially depend on the "modern" view of scholarship and its subject-matter that began in the eighteenth-century "Enlightenment," though it has since taken many turns. The French post-modern philosopher François Lyotard perceived two "metanarratives," as he called them, in modernism: the narrative of progress, and the narrative of the unity of knowledge.[2] This means, first, the assumption that knowledge, scholarly skills, and the world generally, are becoming more and more perfected all the time; and second, that as this happens, we can look at even such human phenomena as myth and literature "scientifically." We formulate general rules from what seems to occur over and over in them. We assume that particular phenomena are best described in terms of abstract general categories that bring together entities of the same type from across the world, assuming they all have basically the same explanation, just as any animal of the cat type, from lynx to lion, is said to be of the *Felidae* family and ultimately related.

As applied to mythology, for example, Lyotard's approach would mean (a) that we now understand myths better than did the people in the past who actually told them (not to mention that we now understand better what the myth was supposed to be explaining), and (b) that this understanding is best put in such general categories as saying, "This is a fertility myth," or "That's a myth dealing with polarities or opposites."

Many of the first Age of Reason or Enlightenment interpretations of myth were essentially Euhemerist, but took new turns in the nineteenth and early twentieth centuries. These modern twists on the old school will be presented first in the discussion that follows. Then we will focus especially on Structuralist, Functionalist, and Psychoanalytic interpretations of myth. These last seem to me to represent the late "modern" heritage of the Enlightenment in myth-studies, even though they, notably the psychoanalytic, almost undercut the Age of Reason as they look for irrational, subconsciousness causations. But it is the rational mind that's doing the looking, and all these schools take for granted that the particular – the overwhelmingly vast array of individual myths from innumerable local tribes and cultures – are to be explained through abstract language generated in the latest stage of intellectual progress.

The scientific-explanatory mind of the last two centuries tended initially to look for a single original explanation of a myth, perhaps of all myth. It pondered myth in parallelism to the Darwinian evolutionary project, which offered the model of moving from very simple origins to more and more complex sequels. In religious studies, the "search for origins" long tried to find a single, simple starting-point for all religion's manifold forms: taboo, totemism, and dreams were proposed. Narrowing the quest down to myth, Edward Burnet Tylor, considered the father of modern anthropology, perceived one origin of myth in dreams. The great Sanskritist Max Müller was convinced that all myth derived from "solar myth," poetic description of the sun's progress across the sky and through the year; gods and goddess were no more than a "disease of language," by which once impersonal poetic accounts of solar events became personalized.

Sir James Frazer (1854–1941), author of the multi-volume and highly influential The Golden Bough, traced religion and the myths and rituals that go with it back to fertility sacrifices, beginning with the killing of a sacred king whose vitality makes the land blossom, and who must therefore be replaced by a fresh candidate once his powers begin to wane.[3] Frazer's work, though always fascinating, is not well-regarded today because of his tendency to force every myth, however taken out of context, to fit the theory. But he inspired a further movement, the Cambridge Myth and Ritual school, which also considered ritual prior to myth, though in a less forced manner and assuming a wider variety of original rituals. As we will see, it is always important to view myths in their total context, which often involved ritual as well as bardic performance, not just as disembodied stories. A more recent proponent of a ritual theory is René Girard (1923–), who postulates the beginning of religion and accompanying myth in the "scapegoat" or victim, often human, whose death is necessary to re-establish harmony in a society disrupted by discord.[4]

If the single-cause modern Euhemerists tended to assume that a key object meant the same thing in every myth across the world – the sun, a victim, a putative fertility practice – then the Functionalists took the opposite stance. Voiced chiefly by Bronislaw Malinowski (1884–1942) so far as myth is concerned, Functionalism declares that a myth can only the understood in light of its function in a particular society; comparisons with other societies are virtually worthless.[5]

That function would be to help maintain the social system by justifying its key components. "Charter" myths tell why, say, the king has authority, women have certain roles, and festivals are held which, in turn, cement social cohesion and help the society function smoothly, at the same time enhancing individual lives.

Structuralism, on the other hand, tends back to universalism. Basically, it views myth as a kind of language which, like any language, has its grammar. Even though the outer forms of myth may vary considerably, basic structures remain the same. Claude Lévi-Strauss, who compared myth to music, also made linguistic comparisons. Individual syllables, even the sounds of individual words, may have little meaning in themselves; but put them together into sentences and they make sense. So with myth, and for Lévi-Strauss the sense they are trying to make is to reconcile opposites, to mediate the contradictions that confront us in life: nature versus culture, gods versus humans, humans versus animals, men versus women.[6] Thus, to take an example we have already presented, Osiris may be nothing in himself, but put him together with his consort Isis, his killer Seth, and his son Horus, and we have a pattern that reconciles several very fundamental human contradictions: male and female, life and death, fertile and storm-wracked land (Osiris and Seth), older and younger generation, the living pharaoh (Horus) and the deceased pharaoh (Osiris).

Finally, let us consider *psychoanalytic* theories of myth. Associated chiefly with Sigmund Freud (1856–1939) and Carl Gustav Jung (1875–1961), though there were other important figures as well, their concepts were immensely influential in the twentieth century, and still have significant followings.

These theories are of course universalistic, since they assume a common deep-level structure in the human psyche worldwide. This, far more than cultural variables, is what makes myth, though its superficial language may be that of the culture. According to Freud, what is common to all humans is far more basic psychologically than differences. We all had parents, together with the experience of infancy and childhood with them. We all discovered sexuality, we needed objects on which to focus its overwhelming power, and we have dreams.[7]

Dreams, together with some waking fantasies, can provide ways of understanding the effect these factors have had on our deepest levels of feeling and motivation. In Freud's view, myths are like the collective dreams of the human race, reflecting common desires and anxieties from the same source that, individually, come out in personal dreams and fantasies.

The most fundamental drives, stemming from the unconscious driving force called the id, and expressed through the libido or "pleasure principle," is broadly erotic or sexual, and understandably first directed toward the parents. Specifically, it is the desire of the child to unite sexually with the parent of the opposite sex, and to see the same-sex parent as a rival, what Freud called, in the case of the male, the Oedipus Complex, significantly deriving the term from the Greek myth of Oedipus who, unwittingly, murdered his father and had sex with his mother.

One can easily how this Oedipal drive, repressed and denied as it may be in the conscious mind, can nonetheless lead to all sorts of "spin-offs": the "incest taboo" Freud thought was basic to all cultures, fratricidal rivalry between brothers, castration anxiety, intergenerational conflict, the violence which so often is the upshot of sexual frustration, even the building of civilization as a means, so Freud thought, to keep the destructive impulses of the id under control.

Needless to say, these are themes common to myth. As we have seen in the case of the Japanese, Greek, and Egyptian examples, myths are full of incest, hatred between brothers and sisters, and violence between parents and children. Freudian mythology takes this undeniable reality as its starting-point. It endeavors to comprehend why these sex and violence issues, unpleasant as they may be, are basic to myth, and are the common dreams (or nightmares) of humanity. It wants to know what they tell us about the deepest roots of religion and culture.

Mention might also be made of the Hungarian Géza Róheim (1891–1953), a Freudian anthropologist who developed an ontogenetic theory of culture, that is, a way of interpreting a culture, including its myths and rituals, in light of its childraising practices.[8] Like Freud, he considered early childhood experience very basic to character, which in turn created culture and expressed its dreams in the form of myth. The figures of myth and dream, for Róheim as for Freud, are really "projections" or personifications of the drives, fantasies, and "traumas" of early childhood, perhaps beginning (as another follower, Otto Rank, would have put it) with the "trauma of birth," and being cast out, as from Eden, from the "paradise of the womb."

Carl Gustav Jung, a major contributor to mythological thought, was a one-time disciple of Freud who broke with the Viennese doctor around 1912, fundamentally on the ground that the latter's primary association of the unconscious with the sexual drive was too narrow. Jung wanted to look at life, with its symbols and energies, in terms of its goal rather than its origin in the id. That goal was individuation, becoming a full and independent person. For Jung also, dreams and myths were the language of this process. Attaining individuation was represented by the birth of the marvelous child, as in the story of the Nativity of Jesus, and of all other set-apart heroes, many of them half human and half divine.

Along the road to individuation we may meet and recognize other "archetypes," familiar figures though they may appear clothed in the garments of many cultures and religions: the Great Mother, the Wise Old Man, the Hero, the Maiden, the Shadow. To become "inflated" with one of them is dangerous, and can lead to the kind of person who is nothing but a mother or a hero, at least in her or his own eyes. But to balance them off within one's personality into a kind of "mandala," or complete pattern, is to be well on the way to rebirth as a whole person.

Jungianism has become a bonanza for mythologists.[9] Jungian motifs are no doubt as common as Freudian themes in the world's myths. Jung's archetypal figures appear throughout the world: the Great Mother, say, as Isis, the Chinese Queen Mother of the West, the Iroquois Sky Mother, the Virgin Mary. The archetypes provide ways in which myths can help one understand dreams, and find helpful companions on the road to individuation. The Jungian archetypes come out of family experience the same as the Freudian projections, though are not so much based in early childhood. Jungianism has often been taken to lend a more positive meaning to myth and religion than did the older psychoanalyst, though both schools have been criticized for giving universal meaning to mythic symbols and ignoring the specific cultural context.

A follower of Jung who has developed his own school, called Archetypal Psychology, is James Hillman (1926–). This approach emphasizes the distinctiveness of all the archetypes, or "personalities," that arise in the psyche, holding that they should not be suppressed by a single dominant ego, but explored and learned from, recognizing that each, well expressed, is a valid part of the individual. A key to Hillman's view is a principle of the neo-Platonist philosopher Plotinus, "All knowing comes by likeness," and the method developed by Plotinus and his disciple Proclus called "reversion." All things desire to return to their archetype or supreme model, of which they are copies.[10] Put psychologically, this means the aspects of ourselves want to return to their inner original: the goddess of beauty, the god of war, the hero, the maker like Hephaistos blacksmith of the gods, the wise old man or woman. Clearly this view gives much scope to the study of myth as illuminated pathway in that return, and Hillman takes myth – chiefly Greek myth – very seriously as means to self-recognition, self-knowing and healing.

ROMANTIC THEORIES

The Romanticism which succeeded Enlightenment rationalism in eighteenth- and nineteenth-century Europe took many forms, but all were founded on the principle that emotion and creative imagination are as valid means to understanding as bare reason. In mythology, this would mean that the kind of feelings that a myth gives one, and the way it provokes the imagination into new insights, are as authentic keys to its essential meaning, both in its own time and for us, as any Euhemerist, rationalist, analytic (in the Structuralist or functionalist sense), or even psychoanalytic deconstruction.

This use of myth has a long lineage. One could probably begin with the Roman poet Ovid, whose *Metamorphoses* tell the stories of some 225 Greek and other myths in poetic form, including some very familiar ones best known, or even only known, from Ovid, such as Cupid and Psyche, or Pyramus and Thisbe, the latter borrowed by Shakespeare in *A Midsummer Night's Dream*. Ovid, also the writer of charming (and graphic) books on the arts of love, was hardly a profound believer in the deities whose adventures he presented, but he loved to play with the emotions and aesthetic delights his artful telling of old tales could evoke.[11]

In the Renaissance, when much of classical literature was rediscovered, Ovid's *Metamorphoses* was the major vehicle for learning mythology. Indeed, the word myth was used to distinguish stories of the Greek and Roman gods, which of course Christians could not believe in literally, and biblical revelation. Nonetheless, many Renaissance painters and patrons scarcely bothered to conceal their delight in the sensual, uninhibited world of the gods, well testified to in numerous nude paintings of Aphrodite and her kin.

Tension between Renaissance "humanism" and Protestant/Puritan or strict Catholic reaction against it, the humanist imbued with a love of pagan myth and the latter suspicious, long affected views of the classical heritage.

Romanticism as such, when it came, evoked feelings that ran more deeply than literary charm or sensual joy. To romanticists, the imaginative door opened by myth was to the long ago and far away, to the collective consciousness of a people, to a way of life close to the soil and to nature. The first and most influential voice of this approach was that of Johann Gottfried Herder (1744–1803). He noted that myths such as those of his native Germany as well as Greece came out of oral tradition, and were shaped by a nation's language and physical environment. Thus, to his mind, they represented a pure, simple, clear articulation of its spirit. Here begins the tremendously influential modern idea that myths relate truth not just in a literary or proto-scientific way, but go behind all that to embody the primal, almost pre-verbal consciousness of the human race – or of a particular race – in its sunrise years when, to paraphrase Wordsworth, our ancestors were still trailing clouds of glory, and the shadows of the prison house had not yet closed around. They were strong, brave, and direct alike in their passion and their heroism, men and women as they were meant to be, before corrupted by too much civilization.[12]

The idealist philosopher Friedrich Wilhelm von Schelling (1775–1854), like Herder, saw myth-making as the profoundest of all human activities. In myth the secrets of original human nature are concealed; they can be unveiled only by philosophy aligned with mythology. For Schelling, myth was a symbol connecting the universal and the particular. When we look for the universal – God, the Absolute, the Totality – we see myth, as if it were like a stained-glass window tinting and giving form to the universal light. When we look clearly at the world all around us, and the stories of all our lives, we see them as myth, in structure and possessing as deep a meaning as the stumbling tales told by the first human children to gaze upon an unspoiled planet. Myth comes first; abstract language is only "faded mythology." Each age, Schelling added, creates its own mythology, not through the pen of individual poets, but through its collective stories.[13]

Another German philosophical name, Friedrich Nietzsche (1844–1900), is also often associated with myth, though in what way seems to be under debate. Was it because of his sometime friendship with Richard Wagner, whose immortal operas based on Germanic mythology clearly presupposed, in the spirit of Herder and Schelling, that myth conveyed veiled truth of immense importance? Was it because in his first book, *The Birth of Tragedy* (1872), used Greek mythology to distinguish between the Apollonian, or controlled, rational state, and the Dionysian, or uncontrolled, ecstatic mind – an exercise certainly in the spirit of romantic mythology? Or was it because Nietzsche endeavored to create his own mythology in such works as *Thus Spake Zarathustra* (1883–5), in which old Zoroaster (Zarathustra) comes back to proclaim the Death of God? In any case, the Nietzschean spirit of pulling radical deep-psychology meaning out of what might have seemed dusty mythological texts was very influential, especially to Freud and Jung.[14]

No doubt the major recent writer on myth most in the romantic spirit is Joseph Campbell, for whom the important thing clearly was the feeling-tinged picture of life and its meaning well-told myth evoked. Though much influenced by Freud, Róheim, and Jung, Campbell was in the end less interested in analysis of myth in psychological terms, than in making its meaning accessible to modern people. But that meant, as it did for Schelling, making of myth a means by which we can see our lives in terms of their largest possible context, the universal itself. Speaking of the "mystical function" of myth, Campbell once wrote it was "to waken and maintain in the individual a sense of awe and gratitude in relation to the mystery dimension of the universe . . . so that he recognizes that he participates in it, since the mystery of being is the mystery of his own being as well."[15] As in most modern applications of mythology at least since Schelling, the emphasis is tacitly but forcefully shifted from the social to the individual, and that is what has made Campbell, as well as the psychoanalysts, relevant.

PEDAGOGICAL MYTHOLOGY

The use of myth as a teaching device, usually of morality or philosophy, has a long lineage, though it may not be particularly in favor today. Plato was the first great example; though he considered traditional Greek myths essentially juvenile and irrational, he was able to use "myths" of his own devising, or editing, to present some of the deepest insights of his philosophy.[16] The most famous example is the Myth of the Cave in *The Republic*. In it people locked into facing one direction in a cave see not reality, but only shadows reality cast on a wall as on a screen; one escapee who managed to perceive the fires shedding the light, the actual objects, and finally the light of day outside the cave was regarded as mad.

In the Middle Ages, Ovid's portrayal of ancient myth was very popular; one common version (in French) was *Ovide moralise* by the Benedictine Pierre Besuire (c. 1290–1362), which offers an edifying moral to go with each of the poet's stories. More recently, myths have been used for political propaganda purposes, and often religious advocates have used stories from out of their own tradition for teaching purposes.

A FURTHER PERSPECTIVE

A recent book by Sophia Heller, *The Absence of Myth*, argues that myth in the sense that modern mythologists have imagined it never existed, since what we call myths were not just stories but parts of total cultures involving total institutions and pervasive symbols.[17] Myth does not exist in the modern world, she says, has not for a long time, and moreover we're better off without it. Of this book, William Doty, himself a distinguished student of myth, said, "At last someone has been brave enough to point out that the emperor has no clothes."[18] Is this wholesale debunking of the mythological edifice right or not?

I have myself raised somewhat similar questions in two places, the concluding chapter of my book, *The Politics of Myth*, and an article, "Is Mythology Obsolete?" in *The Journal of the American Academy of Religion.*[19] I also emphasized that what we call myth is usually not the original myth, but a literary reconstruction of it, ancient or modern. It is therefore considerably detached from the total cultural and religious context in which it had once existed as what Heller considers myth in the full sense, part of a society's culture, public religion, and power structure. Yet by and large the "real" myths of our times, as for Schelling, are not a culture's "official" myths, those learned in church or classroom, but what is in the air, told in the form of out-of-school tales, relayed in the media, so fresh they are not yet recognized as 'myth' or 'scripture.' In our day, think of space travel, environmental apocalypticism, near-death experiences, World War II.

Even the use of the words myth and mythology can be questioned, debunkers say, and here are some of the issues.

(1) The term is too polarized. To some, it means a story that isn't true; to others, a profound truth. Moreover, it is argued that too much mythology has been used to promote partisan positions, including extreme racism and nationalism, and this has left a bad taste. Better get another word.

(2) The definition of exactly what is and is not a myth is too imprecise. This failing can be used against it; Bruce Lincoln, in *Theorizing Myth: Narrative, Ideology, and Scholarship*, speaks of myth as ideology in narrative form.[20] That is not a compliment, since much of his book is devoted to demonstrating a profound relationship between the rise of modern mythology, especially Indo-European, and the ideologies underlying European imperialism and, ultimately, German National Socialism. Many mythologists, of course, devoted their attention to other mythologies – Native American, African, Australian, Pacific – but problems with the term and concept remain. In my article "Is Mythology Obsolete?" I ask if "what is called mythology finally raises questions of exactly what the object of its study is or whether in fact there *is* such an object not really created, like certain quantum phenomena, by the act of observation and interpretation."[21] Do we, in other words, make a story into a myth by calling it a myth and studying it with the tools of mythology?

(3) Talking about myth creates an atmosphere in which those particular stories defined as myth come to have a sacred aura, as though they were revealed truth, for those who want to believe in them. But many "myths" actually were as much humorous or heroic entertainment as solemn faith. One can question whether they were ever "believed" in the way some creedal religions say one must believe the basic articles of faith. Maybe some were just good stories, told mainly for that reason. The many variants of ancient myths suggest that different bards had their own special versions of standard stories, or perhaps even told the same story differently on different days, depending on the audience or the singer's mood; all this suggests that to take so seriously the particular form among many in which we happen to have a certain myth, analyzing it in great detail, is missing the point.

(4) Stories that *were* sacred were used in the special context of ritual and initiatory rites, usually reciting how the ritual was instituted, like the repetition of the words of Jesus at the Last Supper in the Christian Eucharist. Some such stories were associated only with

a particular class or type of person, such as a craft guild or priestly caste. Many were told only at a particular place, surrounded by distinctive art and architecture, accompanied by special music, in the context of a certain rite. Too often theories of myth look only at the words of the story, dissociating it from that total setting. Yet for traditional people, this total setting, an orchestration of symbols in which the narrative is simultaneously received through several senses, is what makes it real; it is not "believed," but experienced – then maybe even half-forgotten, till the next performance. There are people who take church or temple this way today.

In other words, maybe there is no such thing as myth, or at least we could conclude the term has been so disputed, fought over, defined in so many conflicting ways, and so debased in popular usage, as to be nearly useless. In this in may be like another four-letter word used in religion, cult, which once had an acceptable sociological meaning, but now seems for most people to just mean a bad religion, however one define that. (No one calls their own religion a cult, just as no one, unless very sophisticated, calls the stories of their own faith a myth; these terms are used for other people's stories or sects.)

On the other hand, if the word is kept, that would be in large part because there is good in the modern "myth of myth," as it was articulated in the first chapter, and as it was presented in connection with Schelling's philosophy of myth, as symbols linking *both ways* the particular and the universal. These stories, even if we only tell them to ourselves, evoke a special response in a particular hearer, reader, or cinema-seer. They say, "This perception is true, at least for me, and the story helped me realize it." In other words, myth is a meaning category on the part of hearers, not intrinsic to any story in its own right. But if that relationship is defined and understood, the word myth can retain a special value.

This is the view of myth, as stories significant for everyone in the spiritual journey toward meaning, that underlies the work of Jung and Campbell, and more explicitly of the theologian Paul Tillich, whose philosophical inspiration was Schelling. Because these authorities have given myth a meaning many moderns find deeply empowering, albeit on an individual rather than social basis, or within one of the religious subcultures in our highly pluralistic society, the concept of myth may be salvageable despite valid criticism. But that heroic effort would require a sea-change in the function of myth: from primarily a social instrument of cohesion and cultural identity; to what I gather it has become for most modern students of Jung and Campbell, and viewers of mythic movies, a means to individual self-discovery, even of an identity that, at its deepest levels, seems to stand apart from one's environing culture and society. We will return to these matters in the concluding chapter of this book.

CHAPTER 4

SINGING THE WORLD: MYTHS OF CREATION

ENDLESS MIST, ENDLESS SEA

Long ago, before the first children of earth had opened their eyes, or before the first sunrise would burst into glory for them to see, all was emptiness, or as close to emptiness as one can well imagine. For the human mind can hardly contemplate absolute emptiness, or figure how shape or mind could form from nothing at all, like clouds from empty sky. Something there was, though beyond the reach of hand or eye.

Some say it was like a vapor, which finally began to consolidate into mist, and finally after much aimless swirling fell into vague shapes, like those we imagine in clouds. Yet those shapes carried over the energy of their swirling, and in them lay, like the force hidden in a lodestone, all the passion that would take full form only after many sunrises: the desire of female and male one for another, the yearning to make whether from one's loins or one's hands, the anger and jealousy and joy that must follow when the one becomes many, and those many must jostle for space and scope to live.

Others say it was not vapor but endless sea that was first, sea still as a millpond, but so vast that one could sail for an eternity, or perhaps for many eternities, and never reach a shore. Yet on this sea eventually arose a wind, or some action causing whirlpools and, as these vortices coalesced, shapes billowed out from which eye, tongue, and hand would finally bud, and with them the desires by which eye, tongue, and hand would drive a restless world. The first forms turned to each other, and from their progeny, and their progeny's progeny, came a cavalcade of mountains, seas, islands, animals, and finally the race of humans, tiny reflections of their vast but misty parents.

Or it may be the first being awoke, like a fetus gathering its first dim thoughts, to find himself tightly enclosed within a hard case, wherein all was cramped, and dark as midnight in the deepest cave. Restless he twisted and turned, knowing no other, thinking himself master of all, unfit to dwell in such small space. After many ages his struggles had some effect. A crack appeared, and through it streamed something his hitherto useless eyes had never seen: light, bright and golden as only his dreams had before imagined it. He pushed his way out, finally standing upright and triumphant on the broken eggshell, now like a coracle floating on a shoreless sea under the light of immense blue sky. Yet, being master, he wanted more: islands, fire, and above all companions to share his life and do his bidding. The means to these ends, he would quickly learn, were at hand.

Still others, perhaps inland peoples more used to sand and rock than wave, like those who sang the Australian myths already related, recalled endless earth rather than endless sea at the beginning; where it came from they knew no better than others the source of mist or water. But one day, great beings slipped from out of Dreaming, which like all dreaming was not exactly in time as we know it yet which can be remembered, and on this bare land awakened spirit-children, so that they could play parts in the drama of life, before making their own exits back into the Dreaming.

Or could it be that what was first was not endless sea or land but horizonless Mind? Mind like that which holds limited and precarious sway over the kingdoms of our bodies, but which in this case is firm and given all power to execute its commands? Perhaps it was this Mind which sent the winds to ruffle the primal waters, or in whose mighty dreams worlds and even systems of worlds formed and washed away like bubbles on a river.

Yet, just as one could ask from whence came the first water, so do children often ask, "If God made everything else, who made God?" Or must one simply take it as given that there is a gate, like Virgil's gates of ivory and horn, out of which dance the dreams true and false which make the world, but behind which we cannot peer? In any case, our study is the stories the dreams tell. These are the dreams and stories of creation, of the beginning.

MAKING THE UNIVERSE HUMANLY SIGNIFICANT

Any worthwhile human creation myth must bespeak the origin of the world and of humanity in a way that explains the role of humans within it. It must show us what significance we have. The stories we tell about creation say a lot about who, and what, we think we are.

That does not mean humans have to be the main point; in some myths they are, but in others they and their culture seem like an accident or afterthought of the gods. One Chinese story alleges that we humans were first no more than insects which jumped onto the skin of Pan Gu, the primal man out of whose body the world was made. The Greeks said Prometheus stole what technology we have. Or, perhaps we were taught the rudiments of culture by a trickster like the Native American's Coyote. If we follow Prometheus or Coyote, we may be, in fact, only an incident or sport in a larger creation, and therefore, like Coyote, we have to live by our wits, and with what helpers we can find, to get by in a largely alien universe; there are moderns who believe something similar on scientific rather than mythological grounds. Others hold that human life and culture was transmitted to us from the beginning by the highest gods or God out of good will, even if we have sometimes misused these gifts.

It need not be thought, incidentally, that all myths have to be dead serious. Many primal peoples today, such as Native Americans and the African San (formerly called Bushmen), are well known for their ability to enjoy the fun side of life and to laugh heartily at a raucous tale. Our early ancestors surely had as much of a sense of humor as anyone today. Not a few of the myth-stories that have come down to us, like the Chinese insects or innumerable tales of tricksters, could clearly have been played up to great comic effect by a good story-teller.

For all we know, they may have never have been intended to be taken straight. Perhaps the message is, "We really have no idea where humans and their culture came from, so we might as well have some fun with the issue," or, "Maybe our existence really *is* just a joke, so let's just laugh about it." Some societies parade "ritual clowns" at festivals who follow the priests and shamans as they enact their solemnities, doing burlesque performances mocking them, thus keeping the light and the heavy in balance. What are we to make of an account like this, from the Inuit people of the Tikigaq peninsula of Alaska?

> First! there was . . . a magical old woman.
> She lived by herself.
> In the dark back then,
> There was no daylight,
> And there was no moon
>
> Things were upside-down the
> People were animals.
> Animals were people.
> People walked on their hands . . .[1]

This strange old woman then chewed burnt lamp oil, and from it began to make the rest of the world.

Other accounts seriously make us humans the main point of creation; there are scientific moderns who act toward other species as though this were the case, as well as religionists who hold the rest of the universe is meant to be only a backdrop to the human drama. Either way, since we are here, it is important for myth or science to show links between the beginning and human society now, and to give what justification it can to the present ordering of human society.

When it came to creation, it was natural to start thinking about origins through analogies with what we know. How do things start now? Through sexual generation, through a process like consolidation or condensation of that which was vaporous or chaotic, out of an egg, by land being dredged out of the ocean, through things growing from the land like plants, through external construction as a carpenter pounds together a box, by simple command on the part of one who has authority. All these models can be found in various creation myths.

The moment of absolute beginning is perhaps the most difficult. How does the story-teller make something come out of nothing whatsoever? In the Western monotheistic religions as they have developed, it is said that before creation only God existed, and he was able to call the created world into being *ex nihilo*, out of nothing. But in most other accounts, perhaps even the Book of Genesis, one of two stances is taken: either the universe is made from pre-existent materials, though they may be totally unformed chaos or void, represented perhaps by waters or vapors; or, as in Hinduism and Buddhism, the universe has existed forever, without beginning or end, but goes through great cycles of creation and dissolution, then creation again out of leftovers from the old universe, which for the most part had reverted to chaos. We will look at creation myths first in terms of this distinction, then from the point of view of the various kinds of creator gods, and of the processes by which further gods and humans appeared.

CREATION OUT OF CHAOS

In the Greek myth of creation as told by Hesiod, first was Chaos.[2] The Greek word "chaos" does not mean everything in confusion; rather, related to the word "yawn," it denotes a gap, an empty space. Into this "yawning" first came Gaia, the earth goddess.

(However, we have explained before that we do not simply go by the earliest known form of a myth, which here would be Hesiod's, as the most authentic, but accept later literary versions through which it further influenced consciousness as just as much "the" myth. In this respect we could look at the form Hesiod's account took in Ovid's Latin *Metamorphoses* (c. 8 C.E.): here we read that, before land, sea, or sky had been created, Chaos was "a shapeless, unwrought mass of inert bulk and nothing more, with the discordant seeds of disconnected elements all heaped together in anarchic disarray."[3])

Back to Hesiod, it is not clear whether Gaia was born of Chaos, or simply emerged. She was the first of the primordial deities who so appeared: others included Tartaros, the underworld, and Eros, sexual desire. Then Chaos gave birth to Night, and Gaia to Ouranos, the Sky; Pontos, the sea; and various mountains. From now on birth from a woman is the normal means of creation, though as yet without male assistance.

Ouranos, however, is male, and as Sky looming over Earth he mated with Gaia. They produced 12 offspring, called the Titans. All was not well, however, because Ouranos would not allow these children to be born, but pushed them back into Gaia's womb. Furious, she conspired with her youngest, Cronos, to frustrate Ouranos. Somehow Gaia gave Cronos a sickle as he hid within her body, and when her partner tried to have sex again, the child castrated his father; he threw the severed genitals into the sea, and from them were born Aphrodite, the goddess of love, or more precisely, of amorous passion.

Ouranos retreated to become the dome of the sky. The Titans then were properly born of Gaia. They in turn embarked on a tremendous spree of procreation, accounting for innumerable of the mountains, rivers, and islands of the Mediterranean world. The rumbling of volcanic Mount Etna, for example, was the rampaging of Cyclopes born of Gaia but confined within that Sicilian mountain. Cronos married his sister Rhea, and their six children were among the most important of Greek deities, the so-called Olympians: the gods Hades, Poseidon, and Zeus, and the goddesses Hestia, Demeter, and Hera.

Cronos apparently had learned nothing from his father's experience. Like Ouranos in his day, he tried to keep this next generation of children from being born, in his case by swallowing them. Their mother, Rhea, worked out a ruse with her youngest, Zeus, whereby Cronos was given a stone to swallow instead, and Zeus was raised secretly on Crete; when he was mature, he returned and induced Cronos to spit out the other siblings. They, together with several of Zeus's own children, became the gods of Olympus, ruled over by Zeus as king; from then on the order of gods remained stable.

Hesiod's often unpleasant account opens itself to several kinds of interpretation. Like the Japanese myth, it makes the world fundamentally biological and sexual in generation. This perception is important because it suggests that, despite appearances, the universe is alive and conscious, in a way similar to ourselves, though on a grander scale. The myth is also susceptible to psychological readings: the generational battle of sons against fathers, with the mother more likely to side with her son, including a highly Freudian castration-anxiety theme.

Much has been made of the similarity of Cronos with the Greek word for time, Chronos; the somber message is presented that Time devours, or tries to devour, all his children. Or, if a historical interpretation is preferred, the war of titans and gods could possibly reflect an ancient struggle between different contenders for supremacy in Greece. All in all, this complex story tell us that, to the ancient Greek mind, the generation of the world was a difficult passage, no less so than a human birth; and was a process within the universe itself, not effected by an outside deity. Creation was the work by gods and titans who were at one and the same time natural forces and sentient beings.

That is evident in their using human means of generation to create one another. If it is not clear where the very first beings, Chaos and Gaia, came from, all that can be said is that they must somehow have appeared, or else the world would not be here at all.

The account by Hesiod does not tell the origin of humans. This work is called *Theogony*, "Birth of the Gods," and that is what it is about. For that matter, it is not the only version of creation; the Greeks seemed to be comfortable with a number of origin stories. Others, for example, involved a cosmic egg.

Back to Hesiod, when humans are first mentioned, they are simply taken for granted, as though they just came with the mountains, rivers, islands, and other features to which the gods gave birth, along with the animals and vegetation. The gods don't need humans, don't really care too much about them, but can get irritated at them. The first mention of humans is in regard to a sacrifice at a place called Mekone, where men (women do not seem to be present yet) had set up an altar to be the prototype of such worship.

When it was time to divide up the sacrificed animal, Prometheus, a titan unusually friendly to humans, tried to trick Zeus into taking a smaller piece of meat to allow mankind the larger. Zeus was not fooled and took fire from humans as punishment for their imperti- nence. The same Prometheus, in the well-known story, stole flame back for our kind, but was chastised by being chained to a rocky cliff, where he had his liver eaten every day by an eagle, until he was rescued by Hercules. Some later authors said that Prometheus was the creator of humankind; we don't know. The gods were relatively indifferent to humankind (so long as their rites were properly done), unless some deity was particularly attracted to a certain human, as was Aphrodite to Odysseus, or angry at one as was Hera at Hercules. We can draw the conclusion that overall divine indifference was a good thing: it gave humans some degree of freedom, and the Greeks developed that gift well.

As for women, according to another book by Hesiod, *Works and Days*, the first was Pandora, whose name means "Many Gifts." Though her charms made her irresistible to men, she was sent not as a benign gift to those of the male gender but to harass them, some say as further punishment from Zeus for man's impiety. Certainly that mission reflects the low view of women characteris- tic of Greek civilization. It was very much a man's world, in which women were expected only to keep house and produce children, it was hoped male. Yet on the other hand goddesses like Hera, Aphrodite, and Athena were powerful, often the protectors of mighty warriors, and not a few heroes had both divine and human parents. (The paradox of low status for women on earth and pow- erful goddesses in heaven is widespread; compare India and Japan.)

Pandora was indeed endowed with many gifts: beauty by Aphrodite, a thievish nature by Hermes, and a jar which contained innumerable evils she was supposed to keep sealed, but which she could not resist opening. Out of it flew the plagues of war, famine, and disease which have afflicted humankind ever since; only Hope remained in the jar as our sole comfort.[4]

FRESH AND SALT WATER

Greek myth, like that just cited, has had a profound impact on Western culture. Virtually everyone educated in that tradition has at least heard the names of those classical gods, either in their Greek forms (for example Zeus, Aphrodite, Hermes) or Roman (Jupiter, Venus, Mercury). Another family of myths that has had hardly less of an impact is that of ancient Mesopotamia and the western Semitic cultures (Babylonian, Assyrian, Canaanite, etc.) because of its influence on the world of the Jewish and Christian Bible. Here is the Akkadian (Babylonian) creation story, according to the text known as the *Enuma Elish*.[5]

At first only endless seas existed, representing primordial chaos. They were divided into fresh waters, personified by the god Apsu; and salt waters, the goddess Tiamat. The two came together and begot more gods in several generations, including Anu, the heavens; Ea, a clever deity who was to displace Apsu when the latter wanted to destroy the next divine generation of gods (a theme familiar from Hesiod); and Marduk, who in turn replaced Ea as mightiest of gods. Like Apsu, stormy Tiamat – dragon-goddess of the salty ocean – now wanted to annihilate the playful young gods, and made various monsters for that purpose. Understandably, the other deities of the pantheon held she must be defeated. But who was capable of that fearsome task? Ea and Anu tried unsuccessfully. Then Marduk raged against Tiamat with the force of wind and storm, split her body apart, and brought pattern out of chaos. He made one half of the erstwhile goddess of confusion the sky, filling its dome with clouds and rain, dotting it with sun, moon, and constellations to regulate time; the lower half he made the earth.

Becoming ruler of all, Marduk turned his attention to bringing order to his world. The new divine king built Babylon boasting a grand temple and palace. He created humans to inhabit the town, and to be slaves of the gods, doing their work for them, especially digging irrigation canals. Every New Year in that great city the Babylonian king, chief of the slaves, confessed his sins and those of his subjects with tears, then ritually took the part of Marduk as he re-enacted the destruction of Tiamat and chaos.

IN THE BEGINNING, GOD

The account in the biblical Book of Genesis also commences with the lapping of endless waves, for an original cosmic sea is a common Middle Eastern theme, and many scholars see the influence of the *Enuma Elish* in Genesis. But in this narrative gods do not somehow just appear out of the chaos, for there is apparently but one God reigning above the waves as they billow in the primordial darkness. (Nevertheless, the divine name in this text, Elohim, is plural, and that construction has puzzled some careful readers.) But the Hebrew creator, clearly independent of the chaos beneath him, first sent his wind or spirit to hover over the waters. He then said, "Let there be light," and suddenly the endless ocean was illumined. He separated day from night. Then, day by day, he likewise called into being the sky; dry land and vegetation upon it; the lights of sun, moon, and stars in the sky; the creatures of the waters; the land animals; and finally, on the sixth day, humankind, male and female, to whom he gave plants for food and dominion over the living creatures of the earth. Then, on the seventh day, God rested, thus establishing the weekly respite of the Sabbath.

This is the stately account of creation in Genesis 1:1–2:3. There is a second account beginning in chapter 2, verse 4 that presents a folksier, more earthy narrative. It tells of God, now named Yahweh, making the first man, Adam, from the dust of the earth, breathing life into his nostrils, and later making his "helpmeet" Eve from his rib. The tale then goes on to the story of the Garden of Eden. In Genesis 1 and 2 we see two stages of the creation account. The second, Yahweh story seems closer to original oral narratives; the first, often called the Priestly account, is literary in style. But, as though to emphasis the importance of literary as well as folkish versions, the Elohim narrative has had an incomparable influence on Jewish and Christian thought down to the present.

These are accounts of creation from out of nothing, or from primordial chaos. We should mention, however, that some myths, generally from preliterate societies, do not seem to be quite able to conceive of the earth as non-existing at all, but tell of immense changes taking place with the emergence of humanity, or at least of their own tribe. The "Creator" should perhaps be called the "Great Changer" instead. Among the Campa of eastern Peru, for example, it is said that at first the earth was in place but its surface was virtually bare but the Campa people themselves. Then the Creative Spirit gazed at them and determined many of them looked more like something else, so he transformed those Campa into trees, animals, and mountains.[6]

CREATORS WHO REPEAT THEMSELVES

Here is another myth, from India. The god Vishnu is sleeping with with his consort Lakshmi on the coiled body of the serpent Shesha ("reminder") or Ananta ("unending'), who floats on the infinite cosmic ocean; the world is then contained only in Vishnu's thought or dream. When it is time to make the world again, the great deity awakes, and a lotus grows out of his navel. Brahma appears on the lotus, and proceeds to make the world anew. When the new heavens and earth are done, Brahma's consort Sarasvati, and Vishnu's Lakshmi and Bhudevi are found. These gods and goddesses rise up to the highest heaven, to reign over the world save when Vishnu descends to earth as an avatar, in human forms like Rama and Krishna, to correct evil and put the world back on the path of Dharma or righteousness.[7]

This Indian created world begins, each time it is repeated, with a paradisal golden age, but gradually deteriorates through four ages to its last and worst state, the Kaliyuga, when people are short-lived and seek only strife and gain. In the end that age dissolves by the corrosive power of its own evil, and all returns to ocean and Shesha, and Vishnu sleeps, till it is time for him to awake and begin the cycle anew. This has happened an infinite number of times, and will again an infinite number of times in the future. Each full cycle lasts a kalpa, a "Day of Brahma," or 4,320,000,000 human years, a figure comparable to those of modern astronomy.

This pattern of an endless cycling of creation and destruction is found generally in Hinduism and Buddhism, though the details may vary. In Saivite Hinduism each world represents a dance of Shiva as Nataraja, or Lord of the Dance. After that great god has gone through his repertoire he starts beating his drum more and more loudly, until the vibrations shatter the earth, it dissolves into chaos, and it is time to start the dance again.

Buddhism puts less emphasis on creation mythology, but has the same overall picture of endless cycles, or kalpas. At the beginning of each, land and light appear out of the darkness of infinite chaos, and beings are reborn from the previous age with karma intact, so each age commences full of evil. So it is that the present universe was shaped by the thoughts, words, and deeds of the inhabitants of the previous universe.

A Tibetan Buddhist myth relates that this accumulated karma formed a wind that swept through the emptiness between the worlds, and gradually thickened to the point it formed clouds. These then rained until the cosmic ocean was spread across the void. The winds continued to blow, churning the ocean into the masses of land that comprise the earth. But the sentient beings that came to dwell thereon were no better, or worse, than at the end of the previous universe; they reflect only the prior condition of the subtle karmic web shaping all that is, seen and unseen.[8]

One entity therein, however, was the bodhisattva, or future Buddha of the coming world. He had taken a vow before the Buddha of the previous world that however long it took, whatever obstacles he had to overcome, he would become the Enlightened One of a new world. Through many incarnations he is purifying himself so as to attain that sublime end. In the case of our historic Buddha, many of these lifetimes are chronicled in the Jātaka Tales, popular in southeast Asia.[9]

In a number of those "training" embodiments the bodhisattva was an animal, a monkey or deer, who heroically sacrificed himself for his troop, thus gradually honing that great egoless compassion which a Buddha must possess. The high point of every world is when its bodhisattva is finally born as a Buddha, as was ours some 2,500 years ago; from then on, whatever outward progress may appear, the planet is spiritually declining until finally it dissolves. At the right time the process takes up again.

In the West, ideas of cyclical creation and destruction have been more common in philosophical than popular religious discourse. They have often played a contrasting role against the creationism of normative Christianity and Judaism. Cycles can be found in Platonism, and in some wings of kabbalistic Judaism. Frequently this cyclism centers around the concept of the "Platonic Year" or

"Great Year," the length of time it takes for one precession of the equinox to be completed, and the zodiac returns to where it was at the beginning of the cycle.[10]

Cyclical creation both Eastern and Western perhaps represents a more philosophical level of thinking, even if still in mythical language, than out-of-chaos. It tries to hold two concepts together. First, it grants that creation out of nothing, by a god who came out of nothing, is untenable. Even a god must have come from somewhere. Yet, on the other hand, some kind of divine creation scenario is necessary, since the world as we know it seems to have had a beginning, and could not have created itself. Hence creation over and over.

HOW MANY GODS?

Creation myths can also be organized by number of participants. Some, like the Babylonian and Japanese, begin with a primal couple emerging out of chaos, or descending from heaven. Often they come to represent sky and earth. A few others, like the Greek, suggest several gods appeared together, eventually pairing off and mating to create more gods and features of earth. In several African myths, two creators, both male, work together on the job.

Other sets of myths have only a single god as supreme creator. This was the case with Vishnu in the account just presented, and of course so it is with Yahweh/Elohim in the Book of Genesis. He may be the only deity to perform the whole creation simply through divine fiat, beginning with the famous words, "Let there be light." Ptah, the first god in some Egyptian narratives, generated the rest of creation from himself with his own semen.

The next stage involves the origin of further gods and humans. This can happen in a number of ways. Perhaps the most common, and natural, is by sexual generation on the divine level, of which we have seen several examples. But it can also be a matter of sacrifice, as of the Vedic god Prajapati who made the world by offering his own body as a sacrifice, dividing it up so that his bone became the rocks and mountains, his blood the rivers, and so forth.

In one Hindu myth Brahma appeared to create the world anew not on a lotus grown from Vishnu's navel, but out of a cosmic egg. The cosmic egg is a widespread theme, found also in China, Finland, Borneo, Polynesia, North America, and elsewhere. In an account from Tahiti, for example, the primal being Tangaroa first found himself cramped within an egg-like shell. Eventually he accidentally cracked it open, and to his surprise found outside a much vaster expanse, and no one to do his bidding. He made of half the shell the sky, and fashioned the earth below of his own body. Then, not wishing to be alone, he formed other gods, including a female consort for himself. Finally he shaped humans to serve and obey him.[11]

Some stories, called emergence myths, center on an Earth Mother. They are especially common in the southwest of the United States and other parts of the Americas. The people, and perhaps all other gods and animate life, are said to have come out of the earth. In some accounts, they grew like plants from the soil. But very often our kind is reported to have emerged through a hole from a world beneath the earth, the equivalent of the womb of mother earth. It was perhaps a rather small hole, for these emergents may first have been like insects or small animals, only later becoming human.

A similar view is that of many Australian aboriginals who, as we have seen, say that a primal being wandering the land begot human souls and left them at sites now called "spirit wells," from whence they would incarnate at the right time; these are often indicated by rock paintings. The earth itself seemed too great for mere humans to explain, but its features and creatures can be attributed to the ancestors, who went through the land singing them into existence; these paths are the "songlines" by which people today, singing the same songs, the songs of their particular clan, its totem and sacred places, walk to recover contact with the Dreamtime and its creators. This perspective led to a particular view of the earth much at variance with that of other peoples.

Bruce Chatwin, in *Songlines*, tells us:

> The aboriginals had an earthbound philosophy. The earth gave life to a man; gave him his food, language, and intelligence, and the earth took him back when he died. A man's "own country," even an empty stretch of spinifex, was itself a sacred ikon that must remain unscarred . . . To wound the earth . . . is to wound yourself, and if others wound the earth, they are wounding you. The land should be left untouched: as it was in the Dreamtime when the Ancestors sang the world into existence . . . The Aboriginals . . . were a people who trod slightly over the earth; and the less they took from the earth, the less they had to give in return . . .[12]

Among the Iroquois, the earth-creator was a woman, Sky Mother. The story begins in the Sky World, which had already been created. In the center of that world stood a great tree, forbidden to the touch of anyone except the supreme Father. But one day, whether at the command of the ruler or out of curiosity, Sky Mother, who was pregnant, tore the soil away around its roots, and found that they extended all the way down to a hole, opening onto she knew not what beneath the Sky World. She fell through the hole, and found herself in a realm covered with clouds and water. She landed on the back of a great turtle floating on the sea.

Sky Mother wanted to plant crops on the turtle's back, but had only bits of soil and seed with her. Several creatures of the sea told her the only source of more soil was at the bottom of the waters. They offered to dive and bring it up. The duck, the beaver, and other water animals tried but were unsuccessful, some floating up dead. But the muskrat, knowing the way, found soil and brought it to her. Eventually the turtle's back became Turtle Island, a Native name for the continent.

In the meantime, Sky Mother gave birth to a daughter, who in turn was impregnated by the West Wind and conceived twins. They quarreled in her womb, and finally the left-handed twin, refusing to be born in the normal way, burst out of her armpit, killing his mother. After this traumatic event, Sky Mother transformed into Corn Mother, source of corn, beans, and squash, the basic crops of the Iroquois.

The two brothers, Right-Hand Twin and Left-Hand Twin, continued the work of creation. Right-Hand Twin made everything that is beautiful: rolling hills, lakes, flowers, gentle animals. Left-Hand Twin made everything that is otherwise: jagged cliffs, thorns, rampaging rivers, predator animals. Right-Hand was always truthful and goodhearted; Left-Hand full of lies, violence, and crime.

Right-Hand made human beings, so their nature is ultimately good. But Left-Hand insisted on bestowing his gifts too, and introduced humans to sorcery, cruelty, and aggression. Ultimately Right-Hand killed his brother, perhaps finally accessing the stored-up vengeance of the meek. He tossed Left-Hand's body over the edge of the world, into the next level down, the underworld. But Sky Grandmother was angry, and threw the dead twin's head into the sky, where it became the moon. Now Right-Hand rules the day, and Left-Hand the night and the underworld.

Much is dealt with in a myth like this: Iroquois society's matriarchal bent, the origin of many features of earth, and the existence of good and evil. The Iroquois believed these two brothers must be kept in balance; that is expressed in ritual and dance. In festivals, day activities honor Right-Hand; night ceremonies do homage to Left-Hand.[13]

THE EARTH-DIVER

One theme in the Iroquois myth was the "earth-diver," or more precisely "diver for earth," aspect of the creation account. That is a common motif, especially in North American and Siberian mythology. However, the theme is also found in Hindu myth. Here it is, in one of the numerous variants on Vishnu's creation, or re-creation, of the world. Brahma the creator, on awakening from his long sleep on Vishnu's lotus, saw nothing but void and waters around him. Knowing there must be earth under those waters, he produced a boar, Varaha (also considered an avatar of Vishnu) out of one of his nostrils, which immediately grew to immense size, then dived into the cosmic sea. There, in the dark depths, after employing his tusk to destroy a demon who had abducted the earth with his tusk, he found Mother Earth and brought her to the surface. As the goddess Bhudevi she became a consort of Vishnu along with Lakshmi.[14]

A related myth puts the origin of human beings this way: Brahma created his consort/daughter Sarasvati, now a goddess of art and culture, out of his own energy, and then looked amorously upon her. She was so disturbed by this that she ran off in all four directions at once, and to follow her Brahma sprouted the four heads with which he is usually portrayed. Eventually he lay with her, and the offspring were the first man and woman. Two characteristic points appear in this story: that humans have something of the divine nature, and their generation or creation was nonetheless a kind of fluke or accident, or even sin, and so they are far from gods themselves.[15]

Many other stories suggest the same ambivalence. In the Admiralty Islands of Melanesia, humanity was born of turtle eggs left on the beach. A few other myths also have humans equivocally descended from animals: one Tibetan myth relates that people derived from the union of a monkey and an ogress – under instruction of the bodhisattva Avalokiteshvara.[16] The Herero of Namibia have humans coming down from a tree, and the African Pygmies have them emerging from a tree trunk, opened by a chameleon.

We may take a moment to note the almost endless number of folk-tales around the world about the origins of innumerable particulars – places, species of animals, cultural endowments – that enhanced the world of archaic peoples. Often these are attributed to a Trickster, in his role as culture-hero rather than as source of confusion or evil. Thus the previously mentioned residents of the Tikigaq peninsula of Alaska, who live by whaling, say that the low rounded land where they live was once a great whale taken by Raven, their culture-hero who was also a shaman; he turned the immense sea-beast into solid ground.[17] The Tagish people of the Yukon tell how the world was once filled with terrible monsters and giants, who were subdued by their trickster/culture hero, Beaver, helped by his companion, Crow. He killed giants and cut them into pieces; these scraps became useful game-animals.[18] The Saami, formerly called Lapps, say that song was brought to the world by the lovely daughter of the sun, who coming down to earth was distressed to see how glum the people were. So she taught them singing and dancing, and also how the make the bright cheerful costumes of those Arctic people.[19]

THE USES OF CREATION

Myths of creation typically explain several things, in this sequence: (1) the primordial chaos; (2) the emergence of the first gods out of this chaos, perhaps by condensation, perhaps out of a cosmic egg, or other means; (3) the creation, often by generation, of further gods; (4) the production of the earth itself, by generation or by "earth-diving," and of rivers, mountains, and other geographical features; (5) the production of animals and the first people, by generation, awakening, or emergence, and of the genders and basic social usages; (6) the coming of evil; and (7) opportunities for renewal, by means of a universal flood, of heroes, and finally of a vision of a restored world.

The last two features will be dealt with in later chapters. As to the first four, of course exceptions occur, as in the creation by divine fiat of the Hebrew Scriptures. But biological means, whether cosmic egg or sexual generation, is a common pattern. They explain creation in a way that makes sense in terms of the world as observed and experienced by archaic people, and it tells us that human beings have a place in it, however precarious.

It is important to notice how even myths presenting views of creation moderns might consider unsophisticated can suggest a philosophical perspective as well. The Hindu story of a primal god making the world by dividing up his body as a sacrifice brings to mind later Hindu Vedanta thought that says the world really *is* all Brahman, all God, in disguise as it were. But to know God we do not go outside the universe, but look deeply into its, and our own, true nature.

Compare that insight with the Hebrew account in Genesis, emphasizing that God made the world as something outside himself, by decree. In the monotheistic religions stemming therefrom, Judaism, Christianity, and Islam, a very fundamental error would be to confuse the creation and the Creator; one can have a relationship of love, devotion, and service to God, but must not say the world, or oneself, *is* God. To find God one must look beyond the creation.

So it is that some creation myths say we humans may be a fluke, and others make us gods in disguise. We were made by God, but the devil had his hand in as well. Some myths say we may be part earth and part divine, or born animal or even plant, yet awakened to a higher calling. Or they may even suggest that the human condition is so mixed up it is best dealt with simply by humor. Perhaps we have had moments when each of these options made sense.

As you study creation myths, try to put into modern language what they really seem to be saying about the universe and humanity within it.

59

CHAPTER 5

THE HERO'S JOURNEY: THE WARRIOR

Long ago, in the waning days of the Roman Empire, a soldier was riding through an eastern land, a land far older and perhaps wiser than the imperial city on the seven hills, but nevertheless subject to its rule. The soldier's heart was troubled as he made his way amid the green olive groves and grape arbors of this pleasant countryside. For though he wore the short tunic and squarish shield of Caesar's legions, he was sworn to another Lord as well: Christ. Like a growing number of those who dwelt around the ancient Mediterranean Sea in those days early in the fourth century, he was a Christian. But his earthly master, the Emperor Diocletian, had declared war to the death against the Church; all Christians who did not recant would find their faith had cost them their lives.

George – for this warrior was none other than he who would later be titled St George – had no intention of recanting, for he knew the power of his heavenly Lord too well. Soon he would see that heavenly strength manifested anew.

Shortly the legionnaire came upon a city clearly devastated by some horror. No laughter rang in its streets, no song floated upon its air, the haunting look of sadness and dread was in everyone's eyes. Before long the visitor learned this grief was because of a terrible dragon, which so persecuted the populace they were reduced to offering periodically their own offspring to placate the beast's ferocious appetite. The victim was determined by lot. And now, they told George in tear-choked whispers, the lot had fallen upon the town's beautiful princess.

George knew what he had to do. He went forth, and subdued the monster; some say just with the sign of the cross, though others contend it was only after battling the hideous creature with his lance.

The princess then led the conquered brute back to the city with only her belt, or some say a strand of her hair, around its neck.

George offered to dispatch the dragon for good if the city would consent to be baptized; this was done, and he insisted he wanted no other recompense, though naturally some accounts insist he took as further reward marriage to the princess: the classic (though not especially common) hero/monster/maiden pattern. If they were so wed, the union was tragically short, for the hero next went on to Lydda in Palestine, where after gruesome tortures – vividly depicted in medieval illustrations – St George was martyred for his faith in 303 C.E.[1]

Most scholars would agree that death is the only historical event in the legend. But St George and the Dragon is highly significant to mythology nonetheless, for it is a Christianized story that not only inspired much later mythopoetic literature, such as the figure of the Red Cross Knight graphically fighting a dragon and winning a lady in Edmund Spenser's *The Faerie Queen* (1590s), but also stands in a very ancient lineage: Theseus slaying the Minotaur with the help of Ariadne; even earlier, Marduk dissecting Tiamat to make the world.

Further East, in Japan, Susanoo rescued and married a lovely maiden who was to be offered to a gigantic snake with eight heads and eight tales; he accomplished the task by setting out eight full, tempting bowls of sake (rice wine), and when the serpent had drunk deeply of all of them with all his eight heads and fallen into a stupor, Susanoo was easily able to slice him into 80 pieces. And so it goes, right up to Luke Skywalker destroying the technological monster which was the Death Star.

MILESTONES IN THE HERO'S QUEST

In order to get a handle on these stories, we might want to look again at the pattern of the hero's adventured outlined by Joseph Campbell in *The Hero with a Thousand Faces*. It is with some caution that we do so. This is a highly idealized outline; probably no one story has all or even most of these features, and in a few of them the central figure may seem to modern readers more like a bruiser who likes a good fight than a noble character. Others, however, inspire imaginations to this day.

The list has three sections: Departure, Initiation, and Return. Under the first is the Call to Adventure, Refusal of the Call,

Supernatural Aid, the Crossing of the First Threshold, and the Belly of the Whale. Initiation entails the Road of Trials, the Meeting with the Goddess, Woman as Temptress, Atonement with the Father, Apotheosis, and the Ultimate Boon. Before Return, there is Refusal of the Return, then the Magic Flight, Rescue from Without, the Crossing of the Return Threshold, Master of Two Worlds, and Freedom to Live. In the next chapter we will compare the story of Moses with this list. As you study myths of warrior heroes, see how many of these feature appear in them, or are implied.

THE WAY OF THE WARRIOR

In the ancient India of gods and heroes, a prince called Rama was exiled from his palace owing to intrigue, and dwelt simply in the forest with his lovely and devoted wife Sita. But Sita was abducted by the demon Ravana, and taken down to a palace in Sri Lanka. After many adventures, assisted by Hanuman the powerful monkey-god and his forces, Rama succeeded in rescuing Sita. The hero then established an ideal kingship which lasted until it was finally time for his return to the heavenly realms – for Rama was also an avatar or human form of the high god Vishnu.

Beowulf, hero of the oldest major English poem, the great epic of that name, defeated the monster Grendel, and after that Grendel's even more horrific mother. He then reigned 50 years as a powerful and righteous king, able to bring peace to his people. But finally, no longer at the height of his physical prowess, the hero was killed in combat with a dragon even though the beast also died at Beowulf's hand; great was the solemn splendor of his funeral ship, but his state slipped back to the usual confusion and violence.[2]

So it is that when a myth is of an earthly warrior, even though he becomes a monarch, in the manner of Beowulf, Rama, or Arthur, the happy state of affairs is not everlasting. Like St George whose earthly triumph was to be crowned with imminent martyrdom, like all flesh, the hero must leave the earth, and his brief paradise is likely to revert to the world as usual. Indeed, sometimes like Achilles, Hercules, or Galahad, the warrior hero may die, or be taken into the Realm of the Blessed, before it would seem he had lived a normal lifespan.

This kind of mythic hero is essentially motivated by the values of warrior culture, which he supremely exemplifies: these values above all are honor, the sense that he is valued and respected by others; and glory, the way in which his deeds are extolled and retold by others. Perhaps the values of the warrior culture have never been better summarized than in Krishna's words to Arjuna, the great prince in the *Bhagavad Gita*. That mighty poem is really part of a long epic, the *Mahabharata*, about war between two factions of a royal house in ancient India. Arjuna had doubts about going into battle against his kinsmen. But the god Krishna, in human form as the prince's charioteer, reminds him that he was a *kshatriya*, of the warrior caste, and it was therefore his duty to take up the sword of righteousness:

> [T]o a warrior, there is nothing nobler than a righteous war. Happy are the warriors to whom a battle such as this comes: it opens a door to heaven.
>
> But if you refuse to fight this righteous war, you will be turning aside from your duty. You will be a sinner, and disgraced. People will speak ill of you throughout the ages. To a man who values his honor, that is surely worse than death. The warrior-chiefs will believe it was fear that drove you from the battle; you will be despised by those who have admired you so long. Your enemies, also, will slander your courage. They will use the words which should never be spoken. What could be harder to bear than that?
>
> Die, and you win heaven. Conquer, and you enjoy the earth.[3]

(Krishna then teaches Arjuna the way of Karma-yoga, the yoga of action by which he who works or fights without attachment to the fruits of his labor, but only out of *dharma* or duty, is as much united to God as if in the deepest yogic trance or meditation, or as the brahmin lifting hands in prayer.)

It will be noted that these values, honor and glory, essentially depend on the view of others, not on any innate sense one may have of one's own worth or rightness apart from outside opinion. It is for this reason that Krishna was able to emphasize to Arjuna that "People will speak ill of you throughout the ages," and this consideration apparently trumped the prince's earlier lament that he could take no pleasure in the killing of kinsmen, and would rather lay down his bow and die himself than indulge in such evil.

The ancient Greek epic, the Iliad, turns on the "wrath of Achilles," and that great warrior was enraged because his commander, Agamemnon, had taken from him a woman he had won as a prize in battle; for this cause Achilles returned to his tent and refused to fight.

That was not just out of love for the prize itself, but because of the affront to his honor and glory: to his honor because it was a sign he was not sufficiently respected; to his glory because all prizes of war were tokens of a warrior's renown. Thus the commander had in effect stolen from Achilles everything that mattered to him as a warrior.

Some years ago, in *The Chrysanthemum and the Sword* the anthropologist Ruth Benedict made a provocative distinction between "shame" and "guilt" cultures.[4] In the former, a person's sense of self-worth depends on the opinions of others, in the way just delineated. In the latter, it is more internalized. One feels wrong not only because of outside opinion, but also because one knows one has offended against an internal monitor or conscience; one can also feel he or she is right, and thereby know internal self-worth, even though the world be against one. While Benedict's initial application of this distinction to Japanese culture has been criticized, undoubtedly the terms lend some initial insight into the warrior culture of ancient epics – just as it does to the values of the samurai class within Japan.

Clearly, warrior culture and the warrior hero start off with shame-based motivation. But the schema is overly simplistic, and so it is in myth as well. Most of us have something of both within us. Achilles eventually came to question self-assessment on the basis of honor and glory alone. Karma-yoga, which Krishna taught Arjuna after lecturing him on the warrior's honor, could also validate following *dharma* or righteousness even in the face of the opposition of most. Mahatma Gandhi used Karma-yoga as the mainspring of his non-violent struggle for India's independence. On the other hand, few are without some concern for the opinion of others; sometimes the struggle between what we ourselves believe is right, and anxiety about "what others will think," can be excruciating.

As we will see in the next chapter, it is the savior heroes who above all taught inner worth apart from honor and glory in the eyes of others, because their religions especially emphasized the moral and spiritual equation within the individual, rather than as a member of a tribe or group. For followers of the Buddha, Confucius, Jesus or Muhammad, one's karma, virtue, faith, or loyalty was made up by one's own choices, and was directly to transcendent values, not to other human beings.

Nonetheless, the way of the warrior hero can be lofty. We shall now examine it in terms of two models: the *champion* and the *quester*.

THE CHAMPION: HERCULES

The champion is the hero who, like Beowulf, Arjuna, David, Hercules, or Achilles, is a fighter of heroic proportions. He is not identified with a single great quest, like Jason for the Golden Fleece or Sir Galahad for the Holy Grail. He may, like Achilles and his Trojan adversary Hector, be part of an armed force fighting a war, or he may be more or less independent or, like Hercules, involved only in personal obligations. The champion's career may be more like a picaresque: a series of only loosely related events in which he displays his cunning and daring, but which do not add up to a single triumph and reward. Indeed, his character may not always be admirable; he may appear far more concerned about his own honor and glory than for anyone else. He seems instead to be guided by a kind of irresistible fate, together with a love of action for its own sake, more than by any particular goal. This hero does not look far ahead, but puts all his strength and cunning into prevailing where he is engaged at the moment.

It is quite possible that stories of the champion hero go back to tribal hunting societies, or the lonely shepherd, before the era of organized warfare like that on the plains of Troy. The great hunter is, like the champion, more an *individual* fighter, against beasts like Hercules with the Nemean lion, or David alone slaying the lion or bear that sought to ravage his flock; or at best against human challengers to his prowess in field or camp. Even in war, his virtue, like that of Achilles or David, comes out in one-on-one combat. It is noteworthy that, like Hercules or David, the champion hero fights only his equal or greater, never using his power to dominate the weaker, though he may, like St. George, battle on behalf of the powerless.[5]

Even so, the champion's character may not always be admirable; he may appear far more concerned about his own honour and glory than for anyone else. His honor, *arete* in Greek, is masculine virility, and beyond that, supreme excellence, the ability even to exceed himself, to go beyond normal limits in strength and skill. Yet he is human, though "extreme" human, male humanity at the upper edge. Moreover, there is always the danger that his virility, close as it is to violence and the propensity for violence, will darken into overweening pride, rampaging frenzy or, if he is crossed, sullen anger like Achilles'. Many readers of the Iliad find Hector, embracing his wife and holding his infant son before returning to battle, much more sympathetic than Achilles – who was soon to kill Hector – sulking in his tent over Agamemnon's affront to his honor.

The champion's end may come only as the last in a string of episodes, perhaps as tragic defeat after many victories like King Arthur, or he may like Quetzalcoatl of the Aztecs simply sail away (though with the belief he would someday return) or even like Theseus the Minotaur-slayer give up his life only after those who once admired him had turned against him.

The champion hero often is represented as having a special birth, and to enjoy supernatural assistance, as well as sometimes face supernatural adversaries. Not seldom he has a strange but close relationship with a woman, his mother or wife, as though harking back to the days when the women stayed in camp, and the mighty male went out to hunt or herd or fight, but (if successful) always to bring back tokens of victory to the women. Hercules or Herakles was conceived in a union between Zeus and a human woman, thus gaining the enmity of Hera, Zeus' wife. Nonetheless his name curiously means "Glory of Hera", as though his ability to overcome the deadly challenges she put before him somehow added to her own glory. Even as an infant, he displayed his great strength in strangling two serpents she sent to kill him.

As a young man he fought against beasts, Amazons, and centaurs, and aided Jason in the quest of the Golden Fleece. The king of Thebes, in gratitude for the hero's help against an enemy, gave him his daughter Megara as wife. They had several children, but in a mad rage – brought on by Hera – the hero killed them all and their mother. In remorse Hercules went to Delphi, where the oracle told him he could only purify himself by serving a certain Eurystheus.

That individual set the great man to his famous 12 labors, from fighting the Nemean Lion and the nine-headed Hydra, to obtaining the golden apples of the Hesperides in the far west, and descending to the underworld to bring up the three-headed dog Cerberus. After the labors, he was involved in more adventures, and committed acts of still more undue violence, for which he had to undergo further penance, including once wearing women's clothes and spinning like a woman.

Despite his many infidelities, Hercules won the hand of Deianeira, for whom the Champion of the Twelve Labors had to fight with a river god. But Hercules died in a peculiar manner after he shot a centaur, Nessus, who had tried to rape his wife. That dying half-man half-horse told Deianeira that if she soaked her husband's shirt in his blood mixed with his semen, it would keep her spouse faithful; instead, when Hercules put it on, it caused him to die in agony. However, in a privilege very rare for one even half-mortal, Hercules was taken into heaven and became an Olympian god.[6]

Here we see the champion's life as a series of episodes in which his strength, and often his cleverness, is exhibited over and over, but throughout which he does not seem to have changed in any significant way, or learned anything morally or spiritually. At the end as at the beginning, he is living by violence, sometimes excessively, and then fighting to purify himself and for his own honor and glory, not out of pure altruism. Hercules died a death which in Greece would have been considered very shameful, killed (even if unintentionally) by his own wife. Yet he becomes a god, not because of any heroic virtue on his part, but rather out of his great suffering and strength, and no doubt the admiration gods and mortals felt for such an outsize figure, even if flawed.

THE CHAMPION: YI

A comparable figure from China's heroic age is the divine archer, Yi.[7]

Chinese myth, the heritage of the East Asian fourth of humanity today, is largely literary in the form we have it, coming from two Confucian classics, the *Shu jing*, or Book of History, and the *Shi jing*, or Book of Poetry. Far back toward the beginning it posits the Yellow Emperor, Huang di, ancestress of the Chinese people and "culture hero" (giver of such basic artifacts of culture as agriculture and writing) to whom innumerable ancient inventions are attributed. After him came the "Sage Emperors," Yao, Shun, and Yu, somewhere between myth and history.

The story of Yi begins during the reign of Yao, on the day of ten suns. On that occasion, all ten of the suns which ordinarily rise on successive days rose the same morning and afternoon, about an hour apart. As more and more suns filled the sky, each borne by a black raven, the earth below grew hotter and hotter, until crops shriveled, lakes and rivers dried up, and the people were near to death. Realizing how desperate the situation was, the great Emperor Yao prayed to Di Jun, god of the eastern heavens from which the suns came. This deity sent his most valued assistant, Yi, to help.

One by one Yi shot nine of the ten suns with his bow, causing the ravens' black feathers to cover the earth, until only one orb remained in the sky, and temperatures fell back to normal. But Di Jun was angered at the archer, for he regarded the suns as his children, and had wanted Yi only to placate them in some way.

In the meantime, Yi had to deal with still more calamities. First, terrific winds ravaged the countryside. He tracked them back to their source, and with his arrows forced the wind-god to submit. Next he was faced with floods from an overflowing river. He fought with the river-god till he gave up, then – in an episode reminiscent of Hercules – met and married the water-god's beautiful sister, Heng E.

The hero had to meet further challenges: a giant monster, a vicious serpent, a windbird. Yao was pleased with Yi's benefit to the country, and bestowed honors on him. However, his divine master, Di Jun, was not pleased. Still angry at the killing of his solar children, Di Jun told Yi that if he cared so much about the security of earth, he could stay there below as a mortal. The heroic bowman was banished to earth, his divine immortality taken away.

Yi was astounded at such an ungracious reward for his beneficial labors. But he knew what to do. He went to the palace of Xi Wang Mu, the Queen Mother of the West, hoping to obtain from her an elixir made from the peaches of immortality that grew only in her garden.

The Queen agreed to provide the champion with this boon, but only on condition that he first build for her a fine summer palace. This he did, and the edifice sparkled with floors of glass and walls of jade. In return, Yi received a distillation of the elixir in the form of a tiny pill so potent it shone with a soft inner light, and which he was told he must take only after he had prepared himself by meditation. The hero returned home, but Emperor Yao had urgent new tasks for him, including combating a dangerous dragon, so he hid the pill in his house and set out.

In Yi's absence, his wife, Heng E, missing her adventuring husband, was restless. Wandering the house aimlessly, she found the concealed glowing capsule. She took it downstairs and was holding it in her hand when her husband unexpectedly arrived at the door. Panic-stricken, realizing she was probably not supposed to have seen this object at all, she swallowed it.

Suddenly the woman became lighter than air. She floated higher and higher, soaring until she reached the moon. She became Chang E, goddess of the moon, but it was a lonely fate, for she shared the moon with none but a single tree, the hare many see on the satellite's face, and a three-legged toad believe to cause eclipses. And as the moon, renewing itself monthly, is immortal, so was she, though because it meant being apart from her beloved, it was a sad immortality she never wanted.

Yi, disconsolate, appealed to the gods for a way to visit his consort. Their judgment was this: he could once more take his place as a god, but his palace would be on the one remaining sun, where he would lend it a male, yang energy, even as his wife gave the moon its yin femininity. Since the sun gives light to the moon, but the moon gives none to the sun, Yi could visit his wife once a month, when the moon is full, but she could never visit him. And so it remains. China's 2007 moon orbiter was named Chang E after this goddess.

In this tale a champion, through a series of adventures, attained real glory but only ambiguous victory. Though Yi seems more admirable and genuinely well-meaning than Hercules, he still met with setbacks he dealt with as best he could, and both he and Heng E attained a reward they did not want – divine immortality apart – while losing what they did want – life together. So is the lot of the heroic champion, glorious yet in the end melancholy and cursed by unintended consequences, like much of human life.

GESAR OF LING

Scholars have suggested that the name Gesar is derived from Caesar, which somehow made its way from the ancient Mediterranean world to Tibet and Mongolia, where tales of this great king are told. But otherwise Gesar seems entirely native to his forbidding terrain. Here we can only mention a few key points; if all that is related of him by popular story-tellers were compiled together, it would make a book three times the size of the Bible.[8]

Clearly, Gesar fits the model of the mythic hero well. He was born miraculously of a dragon-princess disguised as a poor servant-girl, at a time when the country was in desperate straits from oppression and poverty. But though sent by the gods, the child was ugly and seemingly of bad character. Yet, awakened to his true mission by Padmasambhava, the famous Buddhist missionary to Tibet, Gesar set out to free the land from the tyrants who enslaved it. His countless exploits against evil rulers commonly had three characteristics: he won by cunning as much as by sheer military prowess; he frequently had vital help from a female ally, such as a sympathetic princess in the palace of the enemy; he yearned to withdraw from combat to devote himself to prayer and meditation, and did so whenever conditions were settled enough to permit him to spend a few days away from strife. Finally, when the time came that he could pass care of the land onto the next generation, during a night of vigil atop a mountain he and his beloved queen, Sechan Dugmo, ascended to heaven – or, some say, were transported to the mythical kingdom of Shambhala, land of bodhisattvas and the pure dharma. Gesar was a warrior who, despite many uncertain adventures, seems ultimately to succeed sufficiently to allow himself to "retire"; he is a transition to the next category of warrior hero.

KNIGHTS OF THE QUEST

The other style of warrior hero, the quester, also typically undergoes a series of disparate trials and adventures. But they are conjoined by the theme of a final object: Jason seeking the Golden Fleece, Odysseus striving to get home to Ithaca, Rama yearning to rescue his abducted wife, Galahad and other Knights of the Round Table in quest of the Holy Grail, and in a modern version Frodo driven to destroy the Ring of Power. Thus the story has some degree of unity, and there is opportunity to see the hero in several stages of initiation and self-development as well as meeting successive tests, at least if one read the story in light of a model like that of Joseph Campbell. That is not always easy to do in the original sources, which may be a conglomerate of diverse tales and sound more like a picaresque even though there is a goal at the end. But as we have noted, a myth is comprised of all its variants, ancient and modern. If a modern initiatory and "developmental" reading makes the hero's journey live for modern readers, that is Jason and Galahad as well as Frodo and Luke Skywalker.

THE GREATEST QUEST OF ALL

Let us first consider the most famous of all quests, the quest for the Holy Grail.[9]

Long had a certain portion of England lain under a curse. There all that was green had turned brown, the air hung heavy and dark, and no birds sang. In its center lay a castle which contained a price-less treasure, but its king was sore wounded and did not heal; he was sometimes seen fishing disconsolately in a stagnant lake. This region was called the Waste Land.

One story tells that the land became desolate in this way. The castle was called Carbonek; its ruler was King Pellam. He was a worthy monarch, and the custodian of the greatest relic in Christendom. However, there also dwelt in that stronghold the king's brother, Garlon, a scoundrel who ravaged the borderlands of the realm. A certain one of King Arthur's knights, Balin, quick-tempered and full of rage at Garlon, pursued him to Carbonek, and there slew him. Pellam, not fully realizing who this strange warrior was, attacked Balin, and in the scuffle the latter lost his sword. Panicking, the knight of Arthur ran through the palace, finally breaking into the quiet room atop a high tower.

Here even a man of violence such as Balin felt a strange peace, as though an old and deep magic resided in that lofty chamber, under its deep blue dome and amid its lustrous stones. In the center sat a table upon which rested some object covered with fine cloth, and over it, pointing downward, hung without support a gleaming spear. For a moment Balin stood still, awestruck, as if in the presence of a power greater than he could comprehend.

But only for a moment. Then King Pellam charged in, sword drawn, determined to confront the intruder. Responding like a trapped animal, Balin grabbed the spear and thrust it into the King's groin. The knight felt a burning sensation, then all went dark.

When he awoke, he was outside the castle, lying on the cold ground, and around him all was already beginning to fade and die. Over him bent the magician Merlin, who informed the distraught warrior what he had done. He had violated the shrine of the Holy Grail, where were kept two objects sacred beyond imagining: according to Christian lore, the Grail was the cup out of which Christ had drunk at the Last Supper, and the spear was the weapon which had pierced his side on the cross. Moreover, he had used the spear to wound King Pellam, descendant of Joseph of Arimathea who had brought these relics from the Holy Land to England, and whose keeping he had entrusted to his lineage. Being of such exalted heredity, Pellam was a sacred king bound up with the well-being of his land, and Balin's terrible transgression had put that sacred trust under a baleful enchantment. Only the best knight in the world could reverse the evil, restoring fertility to the land and health to the King, and that mighty deed would be accomplished not by the sword but by faith and the right words.

Many tried but failed. Many knights could not even find the Waste Land and Castle Carbonek, for that strange realm, as though half in this world and half out of it, seemed oddly to appear and disappear; some would see its towers in the mist, others pass the same way and find only brown earth and gray stone. But for long none could approach it.

Finally there rode up to the gates of Carbonek Sir Lancelot, accounted the best knight in the world save for his illicit relationship with Arthur's queen, Guinevere. He was gladly welcomed into the castle and found a lingering splendor still haunting its great hall. King Pellam lay on a pallet, and spoke courteously to the visitor. Then Lancelot observed a strange sight. A silent procession entered the room. Following graceful attendants walked a youth bearing a spear, from which blood still trickled, and a maiden of exceeding beauty holding up an object from which light streamed, but which was covered with a cloth. Pellam told Lancelot, "She who bears the Grail is my daughter."

That night a dark magic took possession of the noble guest in this mysterious place. A serving maid came to Lancelot with a midnight summons, and a ring that appeared to be Guinevere's; he was led away believing he was visiting the queen, his paramour. But with the dawn Arthur's knight awoke to find himself abed with the Grail Maiden instead. Burning with shame and anger, the adulterer rushed from the castle. But his hours with Pellam's daughter bore fruit, a son, and it was that advantageous child who would finally heal the Waste Land.

That child was Sir Galahad, and it was as though he came into the world for this one purpose only. Years later, when he was nearly grown, a youth of exceptional honor and purity, this noblest of all knights was brought by Merlin to Arthur's court at Camelot.

At the Round Table, one seat was called the Siege Perilous, reserved for the best knight in the world. Strange magic, it was whispered, would kill any other who presumed to sit there. Lancelot had always refused, knowing his guilty secret. But Merlin led Galahad directly to it, and when the son of Lancelot and the Grail Maiden (though none but they knew this) seated himself, an inscription appeared on the chair: "This is the Siege [Seat] of Sir Galahad, the

Haut [High] Prince." The Wizard also gave Galahad the bloodied sword of Balin, saying it sought redemption.

Galahad made himself a companion of Arthur's court, training in its ways and easily becoming the best at knightly skills, though he always stood a little apart, characterized by seriousness and an often intense sense of purpose. He was never known to laugh. One evening, as the knights sat around the Table, a gleaming vision appeared in the air: the Grail, which summoned them in audible words to find its high sanctuary, ask the right question, and redeem the Waste Land.

Several set out, each from a different direction. Some would fail to find the query. Lancelot came again to Carbonek, but could not see the Grail. Loyal Sir Gawain saw it, but could only sputter, "Tell me what these things mean."

Finally Galahad arrived, accompanied by Percival and Sir Bors. Sir Percival, who was something of a well-meaning fool, would see the Grail, but that solemn occasion blanked his mind, he could utter no words, and left unsuccessful. But Galahad, in the holy presence of the Grail, bespoke exactly the right sentence: "What is the Grail and whom does it serve?"

It is interesting that the magic did not consist of giving the right answer, but in asking the right question. When it was asked, the King rose, whole again, strong and vigorous. Outside, soft rain began restoring verdant freshness to the land. But, according to some sources, Galahad then gazed deep into the cup, and found there mystery and power too great for humankind, even for the best knight in the world. He died as he looked on the wonder, blissful, his one mission in life accomplished. It was Sir Bors, a soldier unexciting but steady and reliable, who was assigned by King Pellam to bring the message of those great events back to Arthur.

In Galahad we note several common characteristics of the hero: special birth, an older, wise or supernatural mentor (Merlin), a time of training and initiation, the passing of tests (the Siege Perilous, the Question), apotheosis or passing into the divine, bringing back gifts to humanity (the restoration of the Waste Land).

WHEN THE QUESTING HERO IS A GIRL

Let us now turn to a modern example of the quester. Consider Dorothy of *The Wizard of Oz*, famous in both the book by L. Frank

Baum (1900) and the movie (1939).[10] Here is an example, rare in traditional mythology, of a female hero of the quest, and a warrior only in spirit, not of bloodstained sword. Dorothy was an orphan raised by the Aunt and Uncle in Kansas, presented as a hard and barren place about like the Waste Land, where their life was mostly work and the elders never smiled; the one joy in Dorothy's life was her lively dog Toto. Dorothy was carried away by a great cyclone to the wonderful land of Oz, where she had many adventures and killed two witches, though not by intention. Her great purpose, however, was to return home.

When her house came down in Oz, it crushed the Wicked Witch of the East, whose silver slippers (ruby in the movie) Dorothy acquired at the advice of a good witch. This helper advised her to go down the Yellow Brick Highway to the Emerald City and consult the Wizard of Oz, who might know how she could return if anyone could. So, with her animal companion, Toto, the young girl set off, on the way adding three more companions to the traveling party: a Scarecrow, a Tin Woodman, and a Cowardly Lion. They wanted to ask the Wizard respectively for brains, a heart, and courage.

The Wizard, however, deferred, requiring they perform a further labor for him as a test before he granted their requests: bring him the broomstick of the Wicked Witch of the West. That ogress-like woman was a formidable adversary, but eventually the task was accomplished.

However, the Wizard turned out to be something of a fraud or "humbug," who himself came from near Kansas. He could satisfy the three companions with words and symbols for brains, heart, and courage, but Dorothy's return was more difficult. Finally he said he would return himself by the same balloon in which he came, taking her and Toto with him. But at the last minute Toto jumped out of the balloon basket, Dorothy ran to get him, and the vehicle left without them. She was crushed, but after more adventures (or immediately in the movie version) met Glinda the Good Witch, who told her she had the power all along to return using the silver slippers: she needed only to clap them together three times, and express her wish.

This story contains numerous traditional hero-adventure elements, including most of those listed by Campbell: special birth (orphan), call to adventure, supernatural aid, animal and human companions, several dangerous passages and tests of Dorothy's valor, magical flight, meeting with the "goddess," atonement with the father, and mastery of two worlds, Oz and Kansas.

Another heroine to be mentioned again is Rose in James Campbell's epic film *Titanic* (1997). As the great ship is sinking, she descends into its depths – into to the "belly of the beast," like Jonah going into the whale or "great fish" – to rescue her love, Jack, who had been chained there to await his death by the "bad guy." As she makes her way, with water rising around her, lights beginning to flash out, and straining metal groaning like some terrible monster, one sees again a 1912 version of the timeless drama, with the twist that the heroine is saving the hero.

The heroic adventure remained alive in the twentieth century.

HERO'S END

Heroes, both champions and questers, come to varied ends. Some, like Hercules, are happily divinized into immortal gods after death, or like Galahad and Rama attain a blessed immortality with God. Others, like Yi, may become immortal gods, but less happily, their new role keeping them too much apart from the one they loved as human. Still others, like Achilles in the Iliad, can hope for little more than undying glory in the epics of the future, though ironically that glory is attained only by killing and dying on the field of honor. Still others may arrive at only an unworthy-seeming end, like Jason of the Golden Fleece, who as an old man was wont to go out and gaze at his ship, the *Argos*, once the vehicle of his glory but now decaying on the beach, until one day he was poignantly hit and killed by a piece blown off the rotting hulk. Or, like Dorothy, or Odysseus in the Odyssey, the heroine or hero may simply accomplish the goal of getting home, and (although there were later sequels) in the original tale were simply left there to live happily ever.

Theseus, the minotaur-slayer, through long years of kingship grew old and cranky, and was finally killed while trying to escape from a popular uprising against his rule. In the Odyssey the Greek hero Odysseus's clever rhetorical skills, including artful lying, seem to be accepted or even admired. But later Greek writers, and especially Romans, were uncomfortable with them, so that Odysseus became almost a byword for a slippery and untrustworthy character. In the 2007 movie, *Beowulf*, the hero of that name accomplishes his great and oft-sung feat of killing the monster Grendel, but then is bedazzled into striking a bargain with Grendel's enchantress-mother, leading finally to his unhappiness and downfall.

It may be that the champion suffers a death which is tragic yet memorable, like that of Roland, the knight of Charlemagne sung in medieval French epic, who held off a Moorish army before finally falling, having out of pride held off too long blowing the horn that would have summoned help. Like him, and Beowulf, not a few heroes, perhaps weakened by age, are finally defeated, though no less honored for that. Arthur, slain in his final battle by his own illegitimate son, was taken by otherworldly beings into a misty realm and, some say, will return when England has most need of him.

So it is that even the greatest warrior and questing heroes must die, and the end may, or may not, be long after their days of adventure and their hour of glory. Perhaps by then the days of their mightiest exploits were far past, even half forgotten by a new generation.

But in the case of another kind of hero, the savior, their death does not go uncommemorated, for it was through their living and often their dying that they fulfilled a great quest, and brought back imperishable gifts to humankind.

CHAPTER 6

THE HERO'S JOURNEY: THE SAVIOR

FROM THE RIVER OF EGYPT TO THE MOUNTAIN OF GOD

Long ago, deep in the heroic age, there lived and labored a wanderer who was to be a champion, a quester, and more. He was not a savior in the full theological sense, but he was the agent of God in saving his people from earthly slavery. Just as he led that people to within sight of a Promised Land he did not enter himself, so he presents us with a vision of the savior-hero even if not quite of that description himself. He was Moses (if historical, *c.* thirteenth century B.C.E.), who guided the children of Israel out of bondage in Egypt, parted the waters of the Red Sea, and received the Law of God on Mount Sinai.

That desert wayshower makes an ideal transition from the hero of the sword and of the quest to another kind of victor. We will look at the life of Moses as presented in the biblical books of Exodus, Numbers, and Deuteronomy briefly in light of Joseph Campbell's "monomyth" of the hero; titles of his stages are in **boldface**.[1]

Even before getting to that schema, we must note the unusual circumstances surrounding Moses' infancy. Most savior heroes, champions like Hercules, or questers like Galahad and Dorothy, were born of one divine parent, or through some deception, or were at least orphans. Moses, it will be recalled, was born to a Hebrew couple when male children of that race were to be killed; the baby was placed in a tiny craft of bulrushes and set afloat in the Nile. There a princess of pharaoh found it, and determined to raise the child herself. Reversing the more common pattern, where the hero, like Arthur or Krishna, was nobly born but taken by humbler foster-parents, Moses was born of slaves but reared in a palace.

The youth found his identity with his people nonetheless. One day he struck and killed an Egyptian overseer cruelly abusing one of his countrymen; when the violent act was bruited about, Moses fled into the deserts of Midian. Here he joined the Bedouin band of a certain Jethro, tending his sheep and marrying his daughter. It was then, when he was far out in the wilderness alone, that the **Call to Adventure** resounded: the young hero saw a bush burning but not consumed, and drawing near heard a divine voice announcing himself as "I Am," and commanding the exile to go down to Egypt, confront pharaoh, and lead his people out of slavery. Moses' first response was **Refusal of the Call.** He protested that he was a poor speaker and without means to convince the mighty ruler of all Egypt, but God responded that his brother Aaron could talk for him, and that he would be given **Supernatural Aid**.

Moses went down, and dutifully told the ruler to let his people go into the desert for religious reasons. Pharaoh declined, but by the hand of God the Hebrew prophet inflicted more and more signs upon Egypt: the plagues, from frogs and rivers of blood to the killing of the firstborn. After that last tragedy, Egypt allowed Moses and his people to leave: the **Crossing of the First Threshold**. The army of the oppressor soon pursued them. It was then that God, by the hand of Moses, parted the waters of the Red Sea, allowing the Hebrews to cross as though on dry land, or like Jonah passing through **The Belly of the Whale**; the waves then came together again to drown the horses and riders of pharaoh.

The journey from the Red Sea to Mount Sinai, the Mountain of God, led by a column of cloud by day and of fire by night, can surely be seen as a **Road of Trials.** The fugitive slaves complained of hunger and had to accept tasteless but nourishing manna; they were compelled to fight with the Amalekites, who would long be their enemies. However, it is not clear anything in this part of the Bible's fundamentally monotheistic narrative corresponds closely to Campbell's **Meeting with the Goddess** or **Woman as the Temptress.** But perhaps the role of Miriam the prophetess in singing the glorious events of the Red Sea faintly recalls the first; the later folly of the Israelites in making a Golden Calf to worship, when Moses seemed to tarry in coming down from the holy mountain, might distantly suggest woman as temptress. The Golden Calf could have been a form, or mount, of Baal, storm-god of the ancient Near Eastern fertility faith, a savior who was buried and rose again annually; his cultus also worshiped the goddesses Ashtareth, Baal's mother, and Anath, his warrior-like and weeping sister/consort; this devotion was later much denounced by Hebrew prophets.

No question that Moses's role on the mountain on behalf of the people betokened **Atonement with the Father**, culminating in something like **Apotheosis** when he was favored with seeing the glory of God from behind as the Lord passed before him, and he received the **Ultimate Boon** of the Law to cement Israel's special relationship with God.

Coming to the stages of Return, we find a suggestion of **Refusal of the Return** in Moses's declination of the offer of God to abandon the faithless Israelites, after the matter of the Golden Calf, and commence a new chosen people of Mosaic lineage; Moses would not betray his first trust. Perhaps there is nothing quite like the **Magic Flight**, for the journey onward after Sinai is as difficult as before, now troubled by thirst and snakebite, the former cured by Moses striking a stone with his staff and a well springing forth, and the latter healed by his holding up a brazen serpent. But one does encounter **Rescue from Without**, as with divine help the people are able to defeat potentates who stand in their way, like Og King of Bashan and Sihon King of the Amorites.

Finally, Moses falls short of the full savior model if the **Crossing of the Return Threshold** is taken to be the crossing of the River Jordan, the frontier of the Promised Land. For though Moses sees that terrain from a mountaintop, he does not enter himself, but rather dies and hands his commission to his disciple Joshua before the people pass over into the ultimate fulfillment of the quest. Thus in only a metaphorical way is Moses **Master of Two Worlds** and endowed with **Freedom to Live**, though in an inward sense certainly he had long held those powers, as mediator between Israel and God, with unique privileges in both courts. He was indeed a prototype of a new kind of spiritual hero, though retaining a bit of the old. More were to come.

A TIME FOR SAVIORS

The period around the fifth century B.C.E. was labeled by the philosopher Karl Jaspers the Axial Turn or Age.[2] This is a time of an important turning of the wheel of history in many parts of the world. It was the age of the first great philosophers in China, India, and Greece, thinkers who probed behind conventional wisdom of tribe and tradition to ask what more can be said about human nature, the nature of the gods, and individual responsibility. It was the time of great Hebrew prophets like Amos and Isaiah who looked beyond ritual religion to call for social and individual righteousness.

Above all, from our perspective this was the time commencing the work of the great founders of enduring world religions: Zoroaster (before 600 B.C.E.), the Buddha (563–483 B.C.E.), Confucius (551–479 B.C.E.), and Laozi (said to have been an older contemporary of Confucius), of Zoroastrianism, Buddhism, and Chinese religion; if the Axial Age can be thought of to embrace the founders of two other great world religions, Jesus (d. *c.* 33 C.E.) and Muhammad (570–632 C.E.), of Christianity and Islam, then it would extend a little more than a millennium. If we include in this time-frame the very important changes going on in the Indian tradition that would become known as Hinduism, inspired by the writers of such texts as the Upanishads, the Bhagavad-Gita, and the Puranas or myths of savior-gods, it is clear that this period, brief in terms of the long history of humanity on earth, precipitated a real religious revolution.

Before then, virtually all religion in the world had been in the archaic tribal or agricultural style, worshiping polytheistic local gods of the type we have noted in the case of early Japan, Greece, Africa, northern Europe, the Americas, and elsewhere. Today, well over half of the world's people are followers of one of three great missionary, transcultural religions, Buddhism, Christianity, and Islam, centered on one God or unitary principle, fundamentally taught through one revelation transmitted through one man who appeared in the context of known historical time, emphasizing individual responsibility for one's ultimate destiny. Or, they are adherents of Judaism or what remains of Zoroastrianism, essentially (if we take Moses to be a revelatory figure in Judaism) founded in the same way.

Likewise, the great indigenous religions of India, Hinduism, and China, Confucianism and Taoism, in the same period underwent a similar reorientation toward universal oneness and individual moral responsibility and, except for Hinduism, toward single individuals appearing in historical time around whom the new teaching is symbolically centered. This is a tremendously important change, one that affected not only the course of world history since then, but also the intimate spiritual, moral, and social lives of billions of persons.

Indeed, since the discovery of agriculture some 10,000 years earlier, it would be hard to think of anything that has more profoundly shaped human life than the work of those half-dozen or so founders of great world religions. They have had far more influence than countless kings or presidents. Needless to say, they and their faiths carried with them, as they went out into the world, myths to go with their importance. Before looking at those myths, however, it will provide important background if we first briefly consider three points: basic characteristics of axial age religions, why they appeared at the time they did in human history, and essential characteristics of a religious founder.

BASIC CHARACTERISTICS OF AXIAL AGE RELIGION

As to basic characteristics, we must again observe, first, that these religions and their founders appeared at a known date in historical time, and at that hour gave the world a new and essential revelation. It was not, in other words, back in a divine age of the creation, or in the "next generation," in an *illud tempus* or mythic era, or even in the remote past of such mythical heroes or savior-heroes as Hercules, Yi, or Krishna. Jesus, in the words of a familiar Christian creed, "suffered under Pontius Pilate," a well-known and quite historical figure of the day. Yet to the eye of faith at the time of his birth, in the language of the Christmas carol, "The hopes and fears of all the years, are met in thee tonight." Here, not "back then," was the crucial event, the pivot of time and history. This event was, in the words of Mircea Eliade, transition from cosmic to historical religion: from religion centered, as is most archaic religion, on such features as the turn of the seasons, sacred mountains and trees, and the "natural" stages of human life, to religion centered on moments in human historical time and its special demands.[3]

Of course human beings do not easily give up what is familiar and important in its own way. Numerous cosmic religion features have been carried over into the new historical faiths. Their main holidays, such as Christmas, Easter, Passover, or the late-spring Buddha's birthday (Wesak or Hanamatsuri), though theoretically based on events in history, have acquired all the symbolism of cosmic religion midwinter or spring festivals, and some even say Wotan has returned as Santa Claus, and an Anglo-Saxon goddess as the Easter Bunny. So it is, as we will see in a moment, that forms typical of older hero myths have been adapted to fit the new kind of hero, the savior and/or founder of a world religion.

Furthermore, we must acknowledge that this concept of history is modern, and that for most people thinking historically has been unfamiliar. To them, anything that happened in the past, above all of sacred importance, in effect happened in a mythic kind of time, to which miracles and all the symbolic accouterments of myth seem appropriate. Even tokens of the creation-myth are not out of place, like baptism as emergence out of waters representing chaos before creation. For the work of the savior-hero is nothing less than a new creation: it restores and makes right what had gone wrong after the original creation, and opens for humankind a way back to that primal state, when we were in intimate right relationship with the divine.

Hardly less important than the savior in history is the written revelation, the sacred scripture. All these Axial Age religions have written texts, like the Zend Avesta, the Bible, the Qur'an, the Buddhist sutras, which convey their message in words on paper rather than the oral transmission of preliterate myths, and are considered divine inspired or dictated, sometimes in a literal word-for-word way. Obviously, this kind of revelation could not have occurred until after the invention of writing.

These books, and comparable Chinese and Hindu examples, invariably put new emphasis on how the individual, through right faith, moral action, and/or meditation can realize oneness with the One who is the divine reality behind the new religion. Whether Eastern karma or Western law and faith, there is individual responsibility and individual accounting. No doubt this is largely a result of the greater complexity of society now, in cities like Alexandria or empires like Rome or China, in which individuality responsibility has to go farther than in the old tribe, and in which people move far more from one place to another. The spiritual focus, in other words, is now on the human person rather than nature or cosmos. So, appropriately, it is now a special exemplary person, walking our streets in our time, who reveals the new dispensation, not an old-time god of field or forest.

If earlier religions found the sacred in the animal, the plant, the sacred king, or the shaman's performance, the new great religions found the sacred in a single person of universal importance, and in a product of cultural development, writing. In a symbolic individual, a particular point in the stream of history, and permanently recorded words, the transcendent appeared to put a grid of meaning over the confusion of life and historical change. That grid clearly reflected changes in human life and society, giving new meaning to what a human self really is.

WHY THEN?

No doubt greatest responsibility of all for Axial Age religion rests with the invention of writing, and the cumulative effect on human historical awareness over centuries of transcripts and chronicles. Not only could scriptures now be written as soon as revealed, but historical records could be kept. Out of this gradually emerged the realization that we do not live in a cosmic kind of time, always close to the day of creation, and in which each year recycles year before, but in one going irreversible historical time, in which things change and do not change back. At the same time, the ancient empires with their histories were rising and falling: Egypt, Babylon, China, the Indian states, Greece, Rome. History happened, and much of it was bad, especially for ordinary people, as plagues came and went, and one army after another marched across the land to conquer and devastate.

This experience, of what Mircea Eliade called the "terror of history," cried out for some kind of escape, another way of dealing with time.[4] Some found it in eschatology, the idea, as in Zoroastrianism, that history is leading up to a grand climax, in which wrongs will be righted and the Good will be seen to prevail. Some sought it in mysticism, like that of the Upanishads, by which one can enter into a timeless, eternal now outside of history. Some found surcease in conservative, nostalgic worship of the old gods despite changing times, like those patrician Romans who continued to honor Jupiter and Minerva up until the end of empire.

But the most powerful antidote to the terror of history was in the religions of the new founders. For they showed that events can happen within historical time which transcend it and point toward mystical release, and toward an eschatological end. But they also show, just by appearing the midst of our days, that life here and now is also worthwhile. Each individual person is significant, because she or he can make choices, as to moral actions or kinds of faith, that make an eternal difference.

WHAT IS A FOUNDER LIKE?

The founder must have, needless to say, a potent spiritual charisma, so that people are naturally drawn to him and say, in effect, "He has something I want to be near." He must be comprehensive, able to reflect several strands of religious life: the teacher and preacher, the meditator or mystic, the organizer of a movement, the stern prophet or reformer and the warm comforter of the afflicted. Models of all this and more will be required in the new movement. He must present something new and memorable, easy enough for the simple as well as the learned to understand, yet not so radical as to alienate those who, despite their unease in changing times, retain links with the religious past. Thus Jesus said that he came not to destroy the law and the prophets, but to fulfill them, and Muhammad made his sacred center Mecca, which had long been a place of pilgrimage. The new teaching, then, is not so different as to be baffling, but just rearranges some pieces on the religious mosaic so that people will say, "This was really true all the time, but we didn't realize it till now," when the pieces fall around the new teacher bringing forth things old and new out of his treasury.

Two further notes: the founder always has a band of disciples, who are initial recipients of his teaching and who come to have important places in his religion's history and mythology. Second, lest we think success is solely due to the founder's charm, the religion inevitably attains its world status through later association with a major empire: Buddhism with the realm of the great Ashoka (r. *c.* 265–38 B.C.E., Chinese religion with the Han dynasty, Christianity with the Roman/Byzantine regimes after Constantine, Islam with the Caliphate.

THE SAVIOR IN SETTING AND STORY

Many other mythic figures beside the few great founders have the savior hero pattern: Orpheus, Baal, Osiris, Krishna, Balder, to name a few. While they may be less historical than the founders, the latter as their stories have developed share mythological themes with these other saviors. The popular Hindu god Krishna, for example, had like most of them unusual infancy episodes: though born as an avatar or "descent" of Vishnu in the palace of an evil king, he was threatened by that monarch, who tried to kill him (like the similar stories of the infant Jesus and Zoroaster), and was raised by a farm family. His subsequent life had three parts: as a divine infant, of whom many charming stories are told; as a youth, in which he was loved by the gopis or cowherd maidens amid the beauties of the garden of Vrindaban, in an allegory of human love for God; and as an adult warrior and king, including his role in the Bhagavad-Gita. Finally his death conformed to the model: he was shot by a hunter in his one vulnerable spot, like Achilles his heel, as he wandered disconsolate because of unworthy behavior by his followers. Lastly came his apotheosis, comparable to the ascensions of Jesus and Rama, to dwell forever in the heavenly Vrindaban, wherein all who love him purely will be reborn.[5]

The historical founders may display comparable features, but they must also live in the context of their historical times and places, rather than in Krishna's virtually timeless mythic realms. Thus Jesus had a remarkable divine-human birth, and was threatened by an evil king, but that adversary is a quite historical figure, Herod. A few pleasant childhood stories are told of him, such as his remaining in the temple to the distress of his parents, and the account of his making clay birds which flew away, the latter found in the Qur'an but not the Bible. He may even have entertained toward Mary Magdalene something of the meaning of Krishna's love for the gopis, if certain Gnostic gospels are to be believed.[6] As a mature man he delivered his greatest sermons, and finally died as a result of betrayal – though his death is given far more significance than Krishna's – and was taken to heaven to reign forever amid his saints.

The Buddha also had an unusual birth, from his mother's side rather than in the usual manner, and flowers and sweet rain fell from heaven to honor the conquering infant. His royal father, knowing he was a remarkable child, sensed that if his heir saw anything of the suffering of the world, he would not be content just to rule over the multitudes from a throne, but would want to teach them the way out of suffering. So his father built for him a vast pleasure palace, surrounded by high walls to keep out any sight of ill, and stocked it with every pleasure a prince could ask for, including dancing girls and an incomparably beautiful wife.

But eventually, at about age 29, he became curious what lay outside the palace walls, and made his famous four trips into the realm of suffering. There he perceived plain evidence of old age, sickness, and death, and he also saw a wandering holy man who manifested a life wholly devoted to the pursuit of truth. Soon after, knowing he could now live for nothing else but finding the cause and cure of this condition. the future Buddha kissed his wife and infant son farewell, and he himself took up monk's garb and begging bowl. As a young man, he had also known, like Krishna, much love from fair women, but instead of seeing in them the face of divine love, he grasped that all such attraction and pleasure is transitory, and turned another way.

After much searching, including the practice of extreme asceticism, the future Buddha sensed the time had finally come. He seated himself at eventide under a fine old tree, he swore by the earth itself he would not stir from that spot till he had attained ultimate enlightenment, and went into deeper and deeper stages of meditation. Mara, his tempter, came to try to dissuade the questing prince from his calling, employing storms, seductions, and disingenuous arguments, but he would not be deterred, and Mara eventually left. Then, as he Enlightened One saw the Morning Star, he attained breakthrough to full consciousness, knowing unshakable equanimity, wisdom, and inner joy. He taught for some 50 years, dealt with at least one threat against his life by Devadatta, a one-time disciple, and then died from bad food given him unintentionally by a follower before entering into Nirvana or Unconditioned Reality.[7]

Like the lives of Moses, Krishna, and Jesus, the Buddha's story exhibits exceptional birth, leaving home in order to fulfill a spiritual vocation, initiation (Jesus' baptism, the Buddha's enlightenment), temptations by the evil one, a period of teaching, betrayal, and after death entry into an ultimate state.

The prophet Muhammad is a little different, since he is not claimed to be divine. (He is an example of what Max Weber called the emissary rather than exemplary prophet: one who bears a message from the divine but is not necessarily an enlightened mystic.[8]) He did not have a remarkable birth, except in a few much later myths, but he *was* orphaned at an early age, grew up as a lonely and serious child, somehow different from other children. As a young man he wandered the hills around Mecca. There, in a cave, Muhammad saw a vision of the Archangel Gabriel, who began delivering messages to him: these came to make up the Qur'an. His wife Khadijah gave him support, persuading him that the messages were important even when he had doubts. Though the Prophet had faced much opposition in Mecca to his preaching monotheism, he changed his fortunes by means of the great journey to Medina, a trek honored as though it were an initiatory passage, called the Hijra. In Medina he had supporters. By the time of his death ten years later, in 632, most of Arabia was under the banner of Islam.[9]

In the prophet of Arabia we see again the familiar pattern: unusual youth, a time of wandering, a significant connection with a woman, an initiatory experience, a time of trials, a triumphant death. What then can be said about the pattern of the savior hero that is generally true and meaningful?

IS THE STORY OF A RELIGIOUS FOUNDER OR SAVIOR A MYTH?

First we should acknowledge those who decline to see the lives of the founders of historical religions to be in the realm of myth. Myth, for them, is at home in preliterate cosmic religion; with the coming of history, myth stops. In my view, this is too arbitrary. If, as we have tried to show, the conventional lives of the saviors follow the convention hero-myth pattern, that could be accounted part of the savior's credentials, and of his power. Indeed, a case could be made that innumerable saints and religious founders down to the present display the same initiatory pattern in their "official" lives.

Part of the problem undoubtedly is the way the word "myth" suggests "untrue," and that is understandably a stumbling-block to followers of the founders' living faiths. But it should be clear by now that in this study we are looking at myth in an entirely different way. Indeed the case could be turned on its head to say that much of the appeal of Jesus or the Buddha lies in the extent to which their lives, in actuality and in historical time, modeled the eternal heroic mold, making theirs the greatest myth of all, making them religious figures that belong fully to both myth and history.

On the other hand, Sophia Heller, in *The Absence of Myth*, declares that the triumph of Christianity dispatched or trivialized the pagan gods and their countless myths, and she does not present that faith's own narratives as powerful, still-vital myths. Contrariwise, this author states that Christianity is not myth because it is "*historical* religion, whereby the one, true God initiated a series of events with a specific beginning, middle, and end," and the world was no longer "ritualistically created anew every year,"[10] apparently along the lines of Eliade's cosmic versus historical religion, as though real myth could derive only from the former.

It is not clear to me, however, how the historical character of the mythic event makes much difference in the practice of the religion, or the practical understanding of its foundational narratives, for the vast majority of Christians, by whom Christian faith is received essentially as popular or folk religion. Consider, for instance, our wonderful yet myth-laden celebrations of Christmas and Easter. By the same token, as should be clear by now, the traditional lives of all these religious founders, as well as not a few later saints, follow the outline of the hero-myth as surely as any figure from the dawn of time, merely transposing it into what is ostensibly historical time.

For innumerable adherents of historical-founder religions, the events around the life and times of the founding, and the faith's "sacred history," have a special quality almost like that of older myth. These are "Bible stories" or "Buddha stories," back in an "Age of Miracles" or the "first Age of the Dharma," when things could happen that do not usually happen today, unless to the eye of deep faith.

Those times and events are thus myth in the best sense of the word even if true, for they are tales that evoke a special, set-apart time, person, and way of being in the world. In the end this realization does not diminish the events so much as give them reinforcement of mythic power.

As the poet Andrew Marvell (1621–78) said of John Milton's *Paradise Lost*, that great work which expresses so powerfully the Christian mythos:

> Messiah crowned, God's reconciled decree,
> Rebelling Angels, the Forbidden Tree,
> Heaven, hell, Earth, Chaos, all; the argument
> Held me a while, misdoubting his intent
> That he would ruin (for I saw him strong)
> The sacred truth to fable and old song . . .
>
> Yet as I read, soon growing less severe,
> I liked his project . . .
> Where couldst thou words of such a compass find?
> Whence furnish such a vast expanse of mind?
>
> ('On Mr. Milton's Paradise Lost', Marvell)

Perhaps we do not frequently say, we do this because the ancestors did it (unless perhaps one counts the Passover Seder). But reportedly many ask, "What would Jesus do?" in a situation of ethical uncertainty, and many millions weekly participate in the Eucharist, in which are repeated the words Jesus spoke when he said, "Do this in remembrance of me."

The word myth is used here in a positive sense, as descriptive of a certain kind of story, without any implication of judgment as to whether it is true or false. One could hold to the theology concerning Christ of the most conservative churches, and still recognize that the Christian story, though it and all that it implies be literally true, functions exactly as any other myth within the communities for which it refracts central meaning.

In the early church, when classical myth and religion were still alive, or very recent memories, it was common to identify Christ with Hercules, or the dying-rising gods of the Mysteries such as Orpheus, or Sol Invictus, the Invincible Sun, of the late Roman cultus; they could all be seen as invaluable *praeparatio evangelica* (in the title of Eusebius of Caesarea's famous book, which researched classical thought in this light), preparation for the Gospel, rather than as rivals, and the role of the story of Christ as "true myth" could hardly be avoided. Presumably whatever can be said about Christ (or, as we have seen, of Moses) and myth can also be said, on the level of the nature and role of their stories, of traditional accounts of the Buddha, Muhammad, Confucius, Laozi, and other founders of historic as well as cosmic religions.

MEANING AND THE MYTH

The myth of a savior hero, assuming his or her story is taken to be myth, must facilitate several tasks. It must establish its central figure as in some sense both human and divine, or at least a genuine human being with a unique relationship to the divine. It must show that he is sufficiently human to require a time of wandering and questing before taking up his vocation in its fullness, and then undergo a significant initiation in which the awesome calling is received or confirmed. Yet he must be sufficiently divine for that calling and his doctrine to be of unquestioned authenticity. The savior must then be given a span of time in which his teaching and ministry are exercised. Finally, when death comes, his last hours must in some way be significant. They need to make transparent the hero's reunion with the divine, and demonstrate his path as the way to salvation for all.

The union of the divine and the human is no easy task. It is not only that the divine power must be, as it were, well concealed within seemingly ordinary mortal flesh. It is also that the divine must be made more serious, if one may so speak, than divinity would be for a god in splendid isolation. A man-god is capable of pathos and tragedy as well as divine delight. Gods like those of the Greeks were in a sense trivial, for all their power, as the many childish escapades in myths of Zeus and Aphrodite make clear. It is impossible to kill them, or even inflict serious wounds on them; no matter what they do, their lives just go on to the next episode, literally forever. So it is not necessary for them to take anything seriously, as though it were ultimately important.

The monotheistic God of Christianity and Islam, or the ultimate reality of Buddhism and Taoism, is more weighty than polytheistic gods who live only for their own amusement, since that ultimate Oneness embraces whatever final meaning the universe holds. Yet still it takes passion and pathos of the human type to make divine power important to humans at the deepest level. For humans must deal with their recognition that all experiences and all decisions stand in the face of death. The alternatives to whatever one decides are lost forever, and one experience may preclude forever another, in the brief time between birth and death. Only a god who knows what this is all about could have supreme significance for humans.

So it is that the savior hero must make decisions despite human uncertainty, must suffer or transcend suffering, and show that *for us* death is all-important yet not the final determinant of the meaning of our lives.

Finally comes the question of changing the destiny of the world. Though the old polytheistic gods, or even some monistic or monotheistic deities, may want to change the fate handed individuals and the world as a whole, it is not always clear in myth that they can. They too may find themselves part of the whole, under karma or, for the most part, bound by the laws of nature and the tides of history. But it may be that at some level, in some way, a human being could make a free decision that decisively changed the course of his or her own life, or even of the world, if human free will is also part of the system. Perhaps a savior/hero could be such an individual. We will consider such issues next in connection with eschatology, the end of things as we know them, and how we humans and the world confront the end in terms of myth.

CHAPTER 7

THE END OF DAYS AND THE LIFE EVERLASTING: ESCHATOLOGICAL MYTHS

This chapter will be divided into two sections. We will first focus on myths involving personal life after death and the realms to which spirits of the deceased make their often difficult way, and then mythic accounts of the wrapping-up of our world and its timestream. The end-of-the-world stories generally came much later, and quite possibly from a single source.

TWO WORLDS

Did human consciousness as we know it begin with awareness of personal death? Was the first human thought a realization that life is finite, rounded by birth and death?

Then, no sooner was death grasped, did consciousness rebel at the idea that only one life, one death, was all there is? The mind, some early philosopher might have mused, is capable of ecstasy (literally, "standing outside oneself"), of deep memory and wide imaginings, of moments of awareness that seem unbounded. Though death may come, of all that abundance would not something be left over? And though heroes and loved ones may die, do we not still see them in dreams, and feel – even fear – their presence at their place of burial, and in their familiar haunts? In shaman's trance, in poet's song, ideas of other destinies for the spirit than oblivion took shape. Sometimes even several simultaneous destinies seemed necessary to meet all the indicators, and some cultures proposed two or even three souls: one to remain near the grave and the family abode; one to go to a world of departed spirits; perhaps one to be reborn in this world.

From this point on, views of the afterlife are quite varied. In some archaic societies, the world of the dead seems very dismal and tenuous. In a famous scene in Homer's Odyssey, the hero goes to the underworld in order to consult the soul of Teiresias, a great seer, as to what he must do in order to return home.

Odysseus was informed that first he had to sacrifice two sheep, for the departed are mere shades flitting mindlessly about until they take a sip of blood. A bit of that fluid of life will restore them long enough to speak to a mortal visitor. By this sanguinary means Odysseus converses not only with Teiresias, but also with such former comrades in the Trojan War as Achilles and Agamemnon (whom he learns was murdered by his wife on his return home), and with his own mother. One can well understand Odysseus's eagerness to depart Persephone's dark and ghostly realm; of it Achilles goes so far as to say that he would rather be a poor man's slave in the land of the living than king over all the dead.

As we have seen, much the same can be said of the early Japanese underworld to which Izanami descended. The Hebrew Scriptures (the Christian Old Testament) offer very little on an afterlife, apart from a few ambiguous passages, and very late material that may have been influenced by Zoroastrianism. In general, God's rewards and punishments are in this life, and the deceased are either simply gone, or consigned to a shadowy Sheol, rather like Homer's underworld, from which perhaps the Witch of Endor called up the ghost of Samuel.

The ancient Israelites' Semitic kinsmen, the Babylonians and Canaanites, held a similarly bleak view of the afterlife. Their dead, confined to a dismal underworld realm, require memorial offerings to restrain them from harming the living. The Epic of Gilgamesh, the most famous example of Sumerian and Babylonian literature, and perhaps the oldest extant written story in the world, relates the hero's attempt to obtain immortality in this life rather than abide in the "house of dust." He seeks help from Utnapishtim, the Babylonian Noah who, surviving the Flood, uniquely attained deathlessness for himself and his wife. That worthy eventually tells Gilgamesh of a plant able to renew youth. But when, though great effort, the hero found and plucked the medicine of immortality, the sacred herb was seized from him by a serpent. Sorrowfully, Gilgamesh realizes that immortality is reserved for divine beings alone, and accepts that mortals must die.[1]

Other ancient cultures had a much more robust image of life after death. The Egyptians are well known for their interest in post-mortem states, though at first they may have regarded immortality reserved for the pharaoh, who was Horus during life and resuscitated as Osiris after death. According to the very early Pyramid Texts, the ruler's spirit joined the sun god Re in his solar ship to sail with him through the daylight skies and pass through the dark underworld at night. Later, as his identity with Osiris became more firm, and the afterlife was opened first to priests and courtiers, and finally to all pharaoh's subjects, the former sovereign as Osiris was judge of the dead.

The deceased first had to pass through a number of hazards on the underworld journey. These mainly consisted of fending off demons. That task required knowing the demons' secret names, plus certain magical spells. All this information was helpfully supplied in funerary texts, together with guiding maps of the underworld. Finally the pilgrim arrived at the throne of Osiris himself, where his soul was weighed against a feather; those who successfully passed this test entered into their reward, while all others were doomed to oblivion.

Notions of the afterlife were, however, no more consistent in Egypt than in most other cultures. While the soul's moral purity, and knowledge of directions and magical formulas, were important, it also helped if the body had been preserved intact; hence mummification. The spirit should also be sustained with offerings, and remembered in prayers. She or he could then share the life of the gods, often portrayed as endless rounds of delightful, sensual partying and lovemaking in a land quite similar to Egypt, with a great river running down its center. In a somewhat more exalted view, the revenant, like pharaoh, united with Osiris, eternal lord of life.[2]

The ancient Celts, especially the Irish, likewise had a lively view of another world. It is the beautiful and magical fairyland preserved in countless legends, where food and wine are plentiful, and with them feasting and dancing, where the weather is always springlike and there is no sickening or dying. This realm is accessible through holy wells, caves, and the barrow-like tombs of the dead. Tales are common that tell the story of mortals who, by happenstance or intent, found their way there, often to learn that a day in the otherworld could count for many years in ours, or the other way around, and that the gold of that world could turn to dry leaves when eagerly brought back.

The Celtic Other World was also to be found in the land of immortals in the Uttermost West, reached in legend by such intrepid sailors as Bron or the Christian St Brendan. In the Christian-influenced folklore of which we have documentation, the Other World was a fairyland parallel to this world, but not officially the abode of the dead. It seems probable, though, that this blessed realm – the Irish Tir na n-Og or "Land of Youth" and the Welsh Annwn – is more or less continuous with the pagan abodes of both gods and departed spirits.[3]

Other peoples too had these parallel, fairyland-like worlds. We have noted the Chinese land of immortals ruled over by the Queen Mother of the West; Chinese in the Taoist tradition also spoke of Pang-lai, islands of immortals in the sea east of China, where white-bearded sages of immense age and wisdom resided apart from the tumult of this world.[4]

The Germanic peoples of northern Europe spoke of two realms for the departed, Hel and Valhalla. Hel, despite its name, is not the Christian Hell, but a shadowy underworld like many others, the destiny of ordinary, nonheroic people.

Much more lively was Valhalla, seat of the Aesir, the war-gods, Wotan, Thor, and their set. The spirits of earthly heroes fallen in battle were brought to high Valhalla by fair but grave Valkyries, goddess-like maidens who pick out those doomed to death on the field of honor. There in Valhalla those valiant souls enjoyed an eternity perhaps only a warrior could fully appreciate: every day they waged great battle, then at sundown the wounded were miraculously healed, and those killed brought back to life, to spend the evening feasting and drinking in the great hall as tales of the day's adventures were told and retold; next day the scenario was repeated. (Another set of gods, the Vanir, were instead peaceful and benevolent in mood, concerned with fertility, bringing sunlight and life-giving rain rather than battle and storm.[5])

By and large, as time advanced, the vision of the afterlife became increasingly positive in ancient times. The Greeks added to Homer's grim underworld the Western Isles of the Blest, Gardens of the Hesperides, or Elysian Fields, where heroes and others of the happy dead could dwell, though at first this site was reserved for only a few. Still later, perhaps under Egyptian influence, Orphism and other Mystery Religions provided means by which a wide range of believers could attain immortality.

Quite often the Other World was conceived as being similar to this one, with its mountains, valleys, forests, villages comparable to those here. Among the Ainu of northern Japan, for example, the other world is like ours but opposite, so that when it is day here it is night there, and vice versa. Some say that souls rotate between the two, being born successively in one, then the other. For many of the Australian peoples, death means going to the Dreamtime, then returning to the Spirit Wells to be reborn in this world.

The transition from this to the Afterlife realm, and one's status there, may entail meeting tests. Indeed, the journey of the soul can be compared to the hero's journey, with its call, its initiations, its road of trials, and its final reconciliation with the deities. We have seen how the Egyptian soul progressed past various obstacles, some requiring knowledge of secret codes. In Malekula, an island in Vanuatu of Melanesian culture, a male soul had to pass a female monster named Lehevhev, who would only be propitiated by the spirits of pigs sacrificed by the deceased in life. This was performed not only in public ceremonies, but also in men's secret lodges, where such offerings, especially of greatly-valued animals with curved tusks, could bestow higher and higher degrees. It was said, however, that a man who had sacrificed at least one such curved-tusk victim would be assured of an afterlife in a cool, pleasant land.[6]

Here, as another example of an afterlife adventure, is the mythic account of the soul's journey to the Other World, according to Thompson River tribes of British Columbia.

The country of the souls in underneath us, toward the sunset; the trail leads through a dim twilight. Tracks of the people who last went over it, and of their dogs, are visible. The path winds along until it meets another road which is a short cut used by the shamans when trying to intercept a departed soul . . . Three guardians are stationed along this road . . . it is their duty to send back those souls whose time is not yet come to enter the land of the dead . . . At the end of the trail is a great lodge, moundlike in form, with doors at the eastern and the western sides, and with a double row of fires extending through it. When the deceased friends of a person expect his soul to arrive, they assemble here and talk about his death. As the deceased reaches the entrance, he hears people on the other side talking, laughing, singing, and beating drums. Some stand at the door to welcome him and call his name. On entering, a wide country of diversified aspect spreads out before him. There is a sweet smell of flowers and an abundance of grass, and all around are berry bushes leaden with ripe fruit. The air is pleasant and still, and it is always light and warm. More than half the people are dancing and singing to the accompaniment of drums. All are naked but do not seem to notice it. The people are delighted to see the newcomer, take him up on their shoulders, run around with him, and make a great noise.[7]

A guide who knew the protocol and geography of the other side, like Hermes in ancient Greece, could be invaluable. Hermes' realms were those of mystery; he was called "the god who is met unexpectedly." He ruled sleep and dreams, and was particularly concerned with boundaries. In this capacity he guarded travelers as they crossed over from one land to another, and he was also psychopomp or guide of the souls to the underworld, which he alone, apart from Hades and Persephone, could enter freely.

Human shamans also have a special capacity to cross the lines between this world and next; note the "short cut" in the Thompson River account used by shamans trying to reach a departed soul. In trance they can guide the traveler on his or her final journey, and they may also enter the shadow world to recover lost and strayed souls; a soul-loss can often be the cause of illness.

Here is a vivid account of how an Inuit (Eskimo) shaman receives his power, in the form of an *angakok* or helping spirit:

The angakok consists of a mysterious light which the shaman suddenly feels in his body, inside his head, within the brain, an inexplicable searchlight, a luminous fire, which enables him to see in the dark, both literally and metaphorically speaking, for he can now, even with closed eyes, see through darkness and perceive things and coming events, which are hidden from others: thus they look into the future and into the secrets of others.

The candidate obtains this mystical light after long hours of waiting, sitting on a bench in his hut and invoking the spirits. When he experiences it for the first time "it is as if the house in which he is suddenly rises; he sees far ahead of him, through mountains, exactly as if the earth were one great plain, and his eyes could reach to the end of the earth. Nothing is hidden from him any longer; not only can he see things far, far away, but he can also discover souls, stolen souls, which are either kept concealed in far, strange lands, or have been taken up or down to the Land of the Dead."[8]

We ought also to mention the persistent myths in many parts of the world of an earthly paradise somewhere just out of sight on this planet, but which a sufficiently intrepid, and favored, explorer might be able to find. El Dorado, the land of gold in the New World, was the goal of Spanish and later adventurers. Central Asian lore is replete with references to Shambhala, mentioned in reference to Gesar, the blessed land of bodhisattvas lost amidst the Himalayan ranges or beyond.[9] In old Russia persistent legends whispered of a Kingdom of God in some far distant corner of the vast Russian Empire, called the Belovode, Kingdom of Opona, the Golden Land, the Land of Chud, where a "White Tsar" ruled truly and justly, and which could be found by those who sought it diligently enough. There were those called Wanderers who made it their lifework to try to find the mysterious paradise.[10]

THE AFTERLIFE AND THE AXIAL AGE

We shall now move on to the end of days, for eschatology – in the sense of strong influential belief that the world as we know it is moving through linear, irreversible time which will culminate in a dramatic culmination – seems to be a gift (or, some might say, curse) of the Axial Age and its "great religions" founded within historical time.

The Axial Age brought renewed interest in the afterlife generally. Cultures where vivid belief in immortality had been minimal before found their faith in the Other World enhanced, especially when those cultures entered the orbit of one of the new world religions; Christianity in Greece and Islam in Mesopotamia.

More importantly, the emphasis on individual merit, preparation, and faith was all the greater as focus moved from the family or tribe to the *individual* as the center of religious meaning. It is the individual who is judged; who goes to heaven, purgatory, or hell; who makes karma and is appropriately reincarnated. While of course some individuals, especially kings and pharaohs, or members of initiatory orders like those of Melanesia, or Mystery Religions like those the ancient Mediterranean, had made an individual journey beyond the circles of this world based on their own status, most had more or less the same experience as they entered the realm of shadows. Now, in the new faiths, all individually had to face a day of personal judgment. Rather than a further boon for those who had good things here as well, a rich afterlife might instead be a peasant's compensation for a lowly present. Even more significant was the way the Axial Age revolution put belief in personal immortality in the context of a wider eschatology.

The fit was often difficult. In Christianity, how does one reconcile belief in individual judgment, entailing individual reward or punishment right after death in heaven or hell, with the also-important doctrine that the dead are not raised and judged until that "far-off divine event," the return of Christ and the Final Judgment? Nonetheless the new emphasis on the Last Day was tremendously important. Its centrality was mainly because it now made history, the course of human time from the first men and women to the final event, one-way and as significant as the also one-way – and to be once-judged – individual life.

All this was reflected in myth as well as in new kinds of religious values. Religion, through the medium of myth, now had to make sense of linear and historical time, of a summing-up judgment at the end, and culmination, of history. As we have seen, sometimes the ultimate view was cyclical, at least in the eyes of the more sophisticated philosophers, in order to fit the eschaton in with a larger picture of the universe as without beginning and end, reflecting the eternity of God.

"End times" were very dramatic. It may well be the case that the end-times scenario was ultimately inspired world-wide by ancient Zoroastrianism, and that it took its origin amid the vast plains, vast horizons, and soaring mountains of Persia. In Zoroastrianism, as we have seen, the third and greatest appearance of the savior-figure Saoshyant comes at the end of the last age; he will defeat evil for good, and raise the dead in preparation for the final judgment. He has been granted unlimited power, at his coming the dead will be resurrected, and will dwell on a new earth free of old age, sickness, and death. A figure like this, often riding upon a white horse, occurs over and over.

In popular Vaishnava Hinduism, the history of each age of the world goes through a declining series of eras, beginning with a golden age and ending with the terrible Kaliyuga, when life will be brutish and short, and which we are said to be entering now. At the same time, Vishnu enters into the world in a series of ten avatars of "descents," to defeat demons and hold off the worst evils. The most recent are best known: the hero Rama, the divine Krishna, the Buddha, and the tenth and final incarnation, Kalki, who is yet to come. Kalki will appear as a warrior on a white horse at the very end of the Kaliyuga, to save those who can still be saved. Then the earth will be destroyed before its next creation.[11]

The warrior-like figure at the very end before the destruction of the world is a common theme. Kalki has been compared to the rider on the white horse in the Book of Revelation (19:11–16). In Islam, al-Mahdi ("The Guided One"), in some traditions together with Issa (Jesus), appears just before the end to restore the observance of true Islam. In his time the entire world is converted to Islam, but upon his death there is some reversion to uncertainty and chaos until the imminent Last Day, when the dead are raised and God pronounces final judgment. It is very likely these teachings, all of Middle Eastern origin, have influenced one another.

In Buddhism, the Dharma, the Buddha's teaching, declines after the high point of each age of the world, the appearance of the Buddha of that age, as the Buddha of ancient India was of ours. But the next Buddha, after many lifetimes of preparation as a bodhisattva, will come at the right time to restore the dharma and, some say, usher in a paradisal era on earth. While awaiting the time of his descent, he resides in the Tushita heaven. Many popular beliefs and causes have clustered around the figure of Maitreya. Devout Buddhists have prayed to be reborn in his time. Radical or revolutionary political movements, like the White Lotus Society in China (a longstanding presence, but most famous for the White Lotus rebellion against the Jing dynasty of 1796–1805) adopted millenarian ideas from the cult of Maitreya and belief in his coming utopia. However, Maitreya, as Mi-lo, has also been portrayed in China as the familiar fat, smiling figure whose happiness and girth suggests concretely the abundance the coming Buddha will bring to a land all too familiar with famine. Many scholars believe Maitreya to have been influenced by the Zoroastrian Saoshyant and the other end-time saviors inspired by him.[12]

In Tibet, myths of a paradisal land called Shambhala have long enlivened stories and scriptures. Somewhere in the north or in the depths of the mountains, this fabulous realm of the Dharma is the abode of bodhisattvas, who incarnate in our world when needed, and is ruled over by a succession of righteous kings, each of whom reigns for about a hundred years.

It is said that the present age of the universe will come to an end during the reign of the twenty-fifth King of Shambhala, to be named Rudrachakrin, in the twenty-fourth century by the Western calendar. In his day an evil tyrant will arise and conquer all the earth except Shambhala. Then Rudrachakrin will go forth – some say riding on a white horse, and with his general Hanumanda at his side – to defeat the forces of evil by his spiritual power. This great victory will be followed by a millennium of peace, when the Buddha's compassion and peace will spread everywhere. (Some pinpoint the decisive year precisely at 2354).[13]

The North European drama of the end of the present age of the world, available only in post-Christian versions, was perhaps influenced in part by that religion. The Valhalla drama of daily battle of the Northerners will end only with Ragnarok, the final "doom of the gods," when after years of terrible winters and moral depravity, the Fenris wolf will eat the sun and run wild, the skies will split, the cosmic tree shudder, the gods fight their last battle, and fire consume all. There are hints that after this catastrophe the world will be renewed, pristine and peaceful, under the good-spirited god Balder.

In Christianity, the world of linear, historical time, running irreversibly from the creation through the incarnation of God in Christ to the Last Day, has been especially significant. Medieval cathedrals often featured a vivid portrayal of that dread event in altar paintings or stained glass; its anxious anticipation was widespread. More recently, movements like Seventh-Day Adventism, in which expectation of the imminent return of Christ is a central feature, have arisen; despite the "Great Disappointment" of 1844, when thousands awaited a Second Coming which did not arrive, the Adventist movement continues to prosper.

In the twentieth century, forms of Christian apocalypticism flourished. These are beliefs, based particularly on the biblical books of Daniel and Revelation, declaring that times would worsen, blasted by "wars and rumors of wars," until the sudden Coming of Christ. "Premillennialism," as the predominant school of modern Christian apocalyptic is called, features belief in the Rapture and the Millennium. It teaches that Christ will first return to call the faithful who will "meet the Lord in the air" – the Rapture. These elect will then dwell with Christ for a thousand years as affairs only get worse and worse on earth. Plague, famine, disaster, and the rule of the Antichrist are scheduled to torment the planet, before the incredibly dramatic reversal of the absolute Final Judgment and the New Heaven and Earth. This scenario was featured in a remarkably successful set of novels, the "Left Behind" series by Timothy LaHaye and Jerry Jenkins (1995–2002).[14]

Glenn W. Shuck, in *Marks of the Beast: The Left Behind Novels and the Struggle for Evangelical Identity* (2005), suggests that while apocalyptic may be off the radar of most intellectuals, it is not pointless and its importance in popular culture in the US must be understood.[15] What apocalyptic does is deal with great issues of meaning, identity, and history in its own language, that of dramatic, spiritual narrative. These are issues which resonate with many ordinary people, confused by a rapidly changing world which leaves many feeling lost in mazes of abstract bureaucracy and technology. Dramas like those of Christian apocalyptic, in which humble believers are finally vindicated to enjoy starring roles in the Rapture and the wars against the Beast, offer powerful compensation. So it is that the power of myth, in the true sense of the word, continues to flourish.

Apocalyptic myth has also flourished in another arena: the political. The two centuries from 1789 to 1989, from the French Revolution to the fall of Soviet Union, could be called the age of the myth of revolution. Factions on both the extreme left and right, accepting the modernist "metanarrative" of progress, acted on the creed that revolution could speed up social progress almost to the span of a day, in one vast convulsion, from old evil to new utopian society, just as religious apocalyptic is like eschatology at top speed. Robert J. Lifton, in his intriguing book *Revolutionary Immortality*, shows how the exhilarating revolutionary experience, although ostensibly political, easily becomes like secular religion, even like mysticism.[16] Another writer, Herbert Marcuse, recalls that in the commune of 1871 Paris, public clocks were shot by enthusiasts to make them stop, as though amidst the euphoria of apocalyptic revolution time was no more.[17]

THE GATE AND THE VISION

Views of the afterlife have always provided particularly vivid examples of Schelling's notion of contemporary myth emerging out of the consciousness of the times, rather than from a particular authority. The next world inevitably mirrors – often in reverse – how life is experienced on deep levels of consciousness by ordinary people. The Middle Ages and early modern times, beset by war, famine, and plague, prior to the emergence of the modern family and something like modern concepts of child-raising, were times of anxiety. An important relationship, source of both security and anxiety, was of the individual to one's lord, in a hierarchy in which God was in the supreme position. It is not surprising, then, that the afterlife should have centered on a final judgment by that deity on each individual, and it should have been portrayed above all as an individual journey to heaven, purgatory, or hell, states of which life here on earth offered ample foretastes.

By the Victorian period, however, the close-knit family was regarded as the epitome of society. Whether in Swedenborgianism, Spiritualism, or popular culture generally in England and America, great emphasis was put on the afterdeath reunion of loved ones, and the restoration of warm family life, in heaven, often at the expense of notions of harsh judgment. One bestselling novel in late-nineteenth-century America was the feminist Elizabeth Phelps's *The Gates Ajar* (1868). Framed around conversation among women who had suffered loss themselves (but whose notions were resisted by pious churchmen), this work graphically portrayed heaven as a place of happy families united forever, dwelling in beautiful homes and countryside, without hint of tears or trouble. Together with its sequel, *Beyond the Gates* (1883), actually set in heaven, the author gave us much detail about food, home life, childcare, and occupation on the other side. Surely a work like this reflects a new myth seemingly emergent on its own.

Like all real myth, the new heaven was not merely disembodied story. Any familiarity with Victorian popular culture reminds one that the new myth was no less expressed through new styles of romantic poetry, in cemetery art, and in the conventions of mourning and funerals.[18]

What do you think emergent myths about death, the afterlife, and the end of the world are today? You might reflect on the popularity of accounts of near-death experiences, interest in reincarnation, and fear of nuclear and ecological disaster.

CHAPTER 8

SHADOWSIDE: MYTHS OF EVIL, THE TRICKSTER, AND THE FLOOD

THE NATURE OF EVIL

What is evil? Perhaps the first thought to come to mind: Evil is that which causes pain and suffering. It causes pain physical or mental, in oneself or in another. For evil is seen in the anguish of a physical wound, and the tears of a broken relationship; in the eyes of an abandoned or tortured child; in a frightened animal.

Perhaps our deepest feeling as we face these awful sights and sounds is that this is something which ought not to be, yet is. So much in the universe suggests harmonious running: the circling of the planets, the turn of the seasons, even the natural process of birth, childhood, aging, and death.

Then another hand intervenes. Not all who are born age naturally, and die peacefully. The child suffers and wastes away, perhaps horribly, long before her time, whether from natural or human causes. Few creatures in this world, in fact, complete their full life cycle, or attain the fulfillment that seems to be built into their genetic inheritance. This includes not only those fish of whose countless spawn only a few reach maturity, but also those human beings who, because of the deep poverty, disease, exploitation and war that afflict all too many fall far short of all they could be.

Over them looms that Other: in the words of the New Testament, the "abomination of desolation" "standing where it ought not." Many otherwise brilliant philosophical systems have floundered because they have been unable convincingly to explain why, in a universe wrought in profound harmony and, many would say, created by grace of a good God, that Other nonetheless rears its head. It is as though evil, precisely because it is that which ought not to be, yet is, defies any attempt at logical explanation; it is the irrational intruding into a realm of light and reason, or a joker laughing mockingly in the midst of beautiful solemnities.

One myth of Evil, then, is that it completes the universe in a grotesque way. It adds the irrational to the rational, pulls in the tragic to the balance out the comic, sets the pitiful alongside the sublime. In that spirit, as we have mentioned, some Native American tribes follow a majestic festival with a performance by "ritual clowns," who burlesque the pompous priests officiating at the first rite.[1]

Whenever out of place, death is the ultimate incongruity, and so the cynosure of evil. Were we immortal, like the Greek gods despite their very human character, we could no doubt straighten out any lapses or disasters over infinite time. Death puts stop to any such plans; it is the final blockage in a life cycle, an abomination standing where it ought not when our dreams are almost endless, but our allotted time is not.

So it is that some myths, recognizing evil's ironic, inconsistent character, have chosen to treat death more as a joke than a tragedy. It intrudes in human life out of some little, almost ridiculous thing that went wrong. If one cannot do anything about it, why not laugh at it instead of weep? This attitude is particularly typical of certain African myths.

LAUGHING AND WEEPING

Bantu-speakers in southern Africa, for example, relate that the High God, after making humankind, sent a chameleon to give them word that in his creative joy he had decided they would live forever. But the chameleon dawdled along the way, getting distracted as he stopped to eat and rest. In the meantime, God considered further, and decided humans ought to die after all. This time he sent the gecko, a speedy lizard who reached people far ahead of the other envoy. Thus death has been our fate ever since.[2]

In Sierra Leone, it was noted by the Limba people that the snake could avoid death, so it seemed, by sloughing off its skin. He emerged from the process looking as fresh and bright as new. The people said that originally God had intended them to be able to rejuvenate themselves the same way. But something went wrong.

Kanu was the creator and High God; he had originally lived on earth among people and animals, but withdrew to heaven because the animals (not people in this instance!) refused to take his advice and stop quarreling. While still on earth, he wanted us and the animals not to die, and made a medicine that would prevent death. He gave part of it to the snake, and it worked for him. He then handed a bowl containing the rest of the elixir to the snake, telling him to take it to the Limba. But the toad objected, saying the snake moved so fast he would spill it. Toad insisted on taking it himself, even though Kanu asked him not to. But he put the vessel on his head, then jumped, and when he jumped the second time it all spilled. Kanu refused to make more owing to the disobedience of the toad, and for that reason all people and animals die, except the snake, who dies only if someone kills him.[3]

THE SNAKE AND THE GARDEN

The snake reference makes this tale reminiscent of a much more widely familiar account of the origin of evil and death, the narrative of Adam and Eve in the Bible. Here we are told that the first humans were placed by God in a beautiful paradise, the Garden of Eden. The primal parents were given only one rule: they were not to eat of the Tree of the Knowledge of Good and Evil in the center of the garden, lest they die.

Then the serpent came, and persuaded Eve that if they ate of that fruit, they would not die, but rather attain wisdom so as to become like gods. Eve took the fruit, and persuaded her mate to sample it as well. As for wisdom, the first thing they realized was that they were naked, so they made coverings of fig leaves, and when God came down, their wisdom made them frightened and they hid themselves.

God, well understanding what had gone wrong, asked Adam about it. He blamed Eve, who blamed the serpent. The serpent was cursed so that he had to crawl on his stomach, and was told he and the woman would hate each other. Woman in turn would suffer in childbirth, and man would have to struggle to grow the food which had once been freely available in the primal garden. The primal pair was cast out of the garden, and now they had no more access to the fruit that would have let them live forever. In the next scene, their son Cain murdered their other son, Abel.

In itself, this scenario seems almost in the realm of African myth. The serpent is simply a mischief-maker, like his kin who stole the skins, and the coming of evil and death appears on the surface to be no more than two very immature (just created!) people following bad advice – a miscalculation with very serious consequences indeed. Traditional Christian theology (less so Jewish) has, however, made this story into a tragedy with vast repercussions, above all as it was portrayed in John Milton's immortal *Paradise Lost*. The serpent became none other than Satan, the angelic rebel against God of whose mutiny Adam and Eve's bad choice was only a reflection, as he ensnared them in his insubordination. The tone darkens as this deed in the ancient garden becomes the first link in the chain of "original sin," or guilt and propensity to wrongdoing that taints all humans from birth. Again, a myth is completed only in all its variants.

The stories of different religious traditions communicate different attitudes toward the nature and pervasiveness of evil. Some view evil as only a superficial flaw on the diamond of creation, saying that the world and human nature are basically good, even telling stories to make the point that what appeared to be an evil event was really for the good. In that great modern myth, *The Lord of the Rings* by J. R. R. Tolkien, the wizard Gandalf says to Frodo of Bilbo's finding the Ring, evil as it was, "Behind that there was something else at work, beyond any design of the Ring-maker. I can put it no plainer than by saying that Bilbo was *meant* to find the Ring, and *not* by its maker. In which case you also were *meant* to have it. And that may be an encouraging thought."[4] For it was Frodo's destiny to take the Ring to Mt. Doom, where it could be destroyed.

Some, however, live more in dread that evil in all its terrible power is still stalking the earth; much there is on every hand that is as it ought not to be, and at best there remain only far-off glimmers of hope and divine goodness.

ISLAM AND AN EVIL WORLD

The two major wings of Islam, the Sunni and Shi'a, embody contrasting optimistic and less optimistic attitudes toward the prevalence of evil. The majority Sunni wing, based on the tradition of the caliphs who were administrative successors of the Prophet, holds to a fundamentally sanguine outlook as the teachings of God were progressively refined by consensus of the faithful and properly followed ("Sunni" means "well-trodden path"), and more and more people were brought into the House of Islam.

The Shi'a, representing some 10 to 15 per cent of Muslims, largely in Iran and southern Iraq, believe instead that leadership was meant to be held by Imams descended from Muhammad, beginning with Ali, his cousin. The Caliphs, in their eyes, were cruel and ominous usurpers. Not only that, but the third true Imam, Husain, a splendid young hero, was killed by the forces of the Caliph Yazid in a great battle at Karbala in southern Iraq, now the site of the greatest of all Shi'a shrines. The death of Husain is a prime example of history which has become myth and ritual, in its own time yet also for all time.

This tragic event is commemorated annually by Shi'ites over ten days during which the faithful weep, cease from bathing, and may even vent their anguish by dancing wildly, dragging chains, and inflicting sword wounds on themselves. On the last of the ten days, the death of Husain is enacted in a kind of passion play, in which not only the battle, but also his dying of thirst as the heartless foemen make sport of him, is poignantly dramatized. Now the true Imam is hidden, but will return as the Mahdi ("Guided One") to bring justice to earth in the fullness of time.

(Perhaps it is no accident that the place of Husain's martyrdom was in the same Valley of the Two Rivers where, millennia before, there was wailing for Tammuz, the ancient vegetation god who died and came to life every year; the myth changed outwardly from cosmic religion to historical reference, perhaps, without emotionally changing so much.)

The Shi'a world, then, far from one in which submission to the revelation of Allah steadily and progressively triumphs, is a darker sphere where treachery and cruelty are all too likely to prevail on the outer plane. Heroes and true prophets of God suffer and die in anguish, while ruthless imposters sit upon thrones; the number of true faithful is small, compared to that of frauds, and the faithful are known chiefly by the fervor of their righteous wailing for the evils of this hard world and the keenness of their hope in God's inward, invisible plans.

Though outwardly historical, the contrasting stories of the opulent Caliphs and the bitter fate of Husain function effectively as myths, articulating in narrative form two different outlooks. Colin Thubron, in his insightful travel narrative, *Shadow of the Silk Road*, has put it well:

So Islam, in this sorrowful tradition, suffered a curious sea change. The Shia sublimated political failure into pious grief and future promise. And the triumphant Sunni, entrenched in Islamic governance and law, were henceforth haunted by a bitter counter-image of themselves, which repudiated earthly authority, and feasted on historic wrong.[5]

EVIL WITCHES

Another very common source of evil is witchcraft and sorcery. In African and Slavic cultures especially, many if not most unexpected everyday calamities, such as sickness, bad harvests, family discord, or cows that stop giving milk, may well be attributed to an enemy, perhaps outwardly a friend or neighbor, who is secretly a witch. Even birds and animals may be witches in disguise. In 1547, a disastrous fire burned much of Moscow; popular opinion blamed it on witchcraft aimed against Czar Ivan the Terrible. It was said that Princess Anna Glinskaia had soaked human hearts in water. The evil aristocrat then sprinkled that water over buildings and then setting fire to them. A male relative of hers was killed by an angry mob in retaliation.

More broadly, Russian witches were said to be able to control weather, and even to steal the light of the moon. They had an inordinate appetite for milk, and could drain a cow dry at a distance simply by sticking a knife into a tree. It was said that one peasant, facing ruin because the milk of his herd was being taken, stood watch one night in his barn. Toward midnight, he saw a cat steal in, then before his astonished eyes turn into a woman, who began milking a cow. The peasant took an axe, and with one blow severed the thief's arm at her wrist. He went home satisfied with his night's work. But back in his house he found his mother moaning in pain, blood flowing from the stump of her arm.[6]

And of course belief in witchcraft led to another evil, the great witch persecutions of Europe and New England in the modern era, when numerous victims, mostly innocent women, were horribly tortured and often burned to death under the accusations of "witchfinders".

THE TRICKSTER

A mythic figure coming somewhat between accident and tragedy is the trickster, well represented by that Native American troublemaker, Coyote. This animal is wily, cunning, ruthless, and unwilling to defer to anyone else, man, beast, or god. He is deliberately rebellious against the benign forces in the universe in a way Adam and Eve, in their naivete, perhaps were not. Coyote is out only for himself, and even his sense of humor has an edge to it, and his "jokes" can be cruel. Yet for all that, Coyote is appealing in his cleverness, his disguises and his ruses, by which he sometimes outsmarts even himself. For all his unscrupulousness and bad conduct, there is something captivating about the gamer's limitless energy and seemingly inexhaustible bag of tricks. People who have made Coyote's acquaintance rarely tire of hearing of his exploits, and Native Americans have enjoyed his tales around the campfire for centuries.

(One can think of Coyote, and most other tricksters, as like Jack Sparrow, played to great effect by Johnny Depp in the *Pirates of the Caribbean* movies. Jack is clearly just out for himself, and sees others mostly as playthings or as means to his own ends. Yet he cannot help but catch every eye and steal the show when he's on screen, with his grin, his good looks, his gyrations and clever ploys; you can't help cheering him on even as you're appalled. The appalling side of the trickster's attitude recalls Mr Bennet's glum comment in Jane Austen's *Pride and Prejudice*, "For what do we live, but to make sport for our neighbours, and laugh at them in our turn?")

Coyote stories are a good example of the mythic story told in large part for entertainment, no doubt in many versions. Such myths are certainly not intended to be believed in any literal or profoundly theological sense even though they may recite of important things: creation, life, and death. Yet such stories, like all myth, do have about them a tone or attitude indicating a way of relating to the world. Are we to laugh or weep at the rocky way the moral universe seems to set up, or simply stand in awe before the first and last things?

In the case of Coyote, the suggestion is that much is wondrous and beautiful about the world, yet the gods, humans, and animals animating it are not always reliable, though always entertaining. They can send currents in contrary directions, and go beyond what was intended. Even so, what can we do but laugh and enjoy the story?

Here is a Coyote story from the Maidu people of California. At the beginning, when nothing lay below but endless waters, two beings looked down and began talking about how the property might be developed, Earthmaker and Coyote. Earthmaker wanted to create a good, respectable world in which pain and death were not,

KEY CONCEPTS IN RELIGION: MYTH

and spouses remained faithful to one another. But Coyote said in effect, "Why not make it a little more interesting?"

He's not exactly evil, and at first he and Earthmaker are not antagonists; the two are like good companions talking enthusiastically about their new project, Earth. But clearly they are of different temperaments. One is straight, well-meaning, but a little dull and unimaginative; the other more interested in angles, and bursting with imagination: more than is called for, and enough to get him into trouble. Clearly the Maidu considered the world offered plenty of evidence for both these personalities at work in its dramas.

In time, Earthmaker and Coyote had a falling out. Earthmaker wanted the people he was making, when they died, to be placed in water overnight and then be able to rise up again the next morning; and he wanted even married couples to be celibate, since there was no need for procreation in a world without death. Coyote said of this:

> But you, Earthmaker,
> are not speaking for human contentment and joy!
> But I speak for a world where men can laugh
> and feel good and come to take delight in themselves
> and in the women they care for.
> So then, an old man,
> flirting and playing around with a young woman,
> should feel like a lad again.
> And women should feel that way too.

Coyote obviously felt that a world without flirting, love, and sex was hardly worth living in, even if the price was death, for immortal life in such a world would be bound to get very boring. To this, Earthmaker had no answer, so

> . . . he thought to himself:
> "You, Coyote, have overcome me in everything;
> so then, without my saying so,
> let there be Death in the World."

But, as happened more often than not, Coyote's victory came back on himself. Not long afterward he sent his own fine son to fetch some water. On that simple expedition the boy was bitten by a rattlesnake, and died.

The Coyote cried out [to Earthmaker]
"May I never say such things again!
You must make my son come back to life!"

But Earthmaker paid no attention, and Coyote, full of anger and remorse as he learned what death meant in personal as well as theo-retical terms, could only say of Earthmaker, "I will chase him no longer . . . I will never catch up with him."[7]
Sometimes the rebel against heaven is a culture hero too, and indeed may be on the human side against the gods, playing his tricks for human benefit. The best-known example is the Greek Prometheus, presented earlier, who though a lower deity or titan was a friend of humanity.
The great drama *Prometheus Bound* by Aeschylus has Prometheus not only return fire but, in the manner of trickster who is also a culture hero, teach humanity such arts of civilization as writing, mathematics, farming, and science. A later story also tells us that at one point in the Bronze Age, when humankind had become very wicked, Zeus raised a flood to destroy them. But Prometheus advised his son Deucalion to build a chest. In it Deucalion and his wife Pyrrha floated out the deluge, which drowned all other humans except a few who fled to high mountains. This leads into another antidote to evil: the flood.

THE FLOOD

The ancient flood by which God or the gods attempt to destroy an evil human race, and only a select few survive, is a common feature in the dramas of evil and its remedy. Noah and his flood in the Book of Genesis is widely familiar in Western civilization. Amidst a wicked generation, only Noah and his kin were righteous. God, determining to annihilate the rest, instructed that godly man to build a ship, the Ark, on which his family and two of every kind of animal (seven of "clean" animals) would be preserved. Rains came and fell for forty days and forty nights, covering even the highest mountains with water.
When finally after 150 days the waters began to recede and the Ark came down atop Mount Ararat, Noah sent out a raven and then a dove to see if they could spot more dry land. The raven circled around finding nothing, but the dove first returned with an olive

branch, then did not return at all. Cautiously Noah, his family, and his precious cargo disembarked, and the righteous man offered thanks to God as a rainbow appeared in the sky, a sign of lasting peace between heaven and earth.

Comparable stories of a universal flood to eradicate evil, or simply the result of a deity's fit of rage, and of a small party who survive, are remarkably widespread across the earth. Examples from Mesopotamia, found in similar Sumerian, Babylonian, and Assyrian versions, are undoubtedly related to the biblical story. The Assyrian and Babylonian forms tells us that the gods, led by Enlil (originally the Sumerian sky-god), wanted to cleanse earth of human overpopulation, but Utnapishtim (the Babylonian Noah) was warned by the benign god Ea in a dream, and with some crafts-men built a large boat: an acre in area, seven decks high. He took aboard his family, the craftsmen, and "the seed of all living crea-tures." Storms then raged for six days, and likewise the waters of the abyss were released, all so fiercely that even the gods were alarmed, and repented what they had done. The boat landed atop Mount Nisur, and Utnapishtim released a dove, which returned, and like-wise so did a sparrow. But then the navigator sent out a raven, and when it failed to come back he knew the waters had receded. He offered sacrifice, and as we have seen he and his wife were, uniquely among humankind, given the boon of immortality.[8]

In faraway China, flooding was an ever-present threat in the days of the mythic sage-emperors, as it has been ever since. This story takes place in the days of the sage-emperor Yao, mentioned earlier in Chapter 6 in connection with Yi and the ten suns. That sovereign turned for help to the immortal hero Gun, a grandson of the Yellow Emperor, the latter, as we saw in that earlier account, a great culture-bearer and now heavenly ruler. But Gun, though compassionate and wanting to help humankind, was nonplussed as to how until he met two strange beings in the form of a black turtle and a horned owl. They told him what he needed was the Swelling Soil, a marvelous bit of earth that would absorb all the water in which it was placed, then spread itself across the fields as rich, moist earth ready for planting. They told him how to obtain it; that magical secret has never been revealed.

However, the Yellow Emperor, looking down from above, was dis-pleased at his grandson's so taking matters into his own hands, and saw to it that immortality was taken away from Gun. Yet the imperial grandson's body did not decompose, and three years later a remarkable thing happened: a new hero, Yu, emerged from the former savior's corpse.

In Yu's day also floods ravaged China, and the emperor Shun, who had succeeded Yao, assigned him to deal with the problem as had his putative father Gun. The latter, not wishing to make Gun's mistake, humbly asked Huang Di's permission to use the Swelling Soil. Pleased at the hero's proper procedures, the high monarch granted the request.

The job was not as easy as might have been expected, though, for Gong Gong, the Water God, felt threatened by Yu's efforts and tried continually to reverse them. As soon as Yu dove beneath the floods to plug deep water outlets with Swelling Soil, Gong Gong washed them open again. Yu was compelled to call all other spirits to join him in doing battle again the powerful aquatic deity. Finally humankind's foe had to withdraw. Then, like the culture hero he was, Yu helped earth's beleaguered people drain off the waters, build channels (in which task he was helped by a gigantic dragon who used his tail as a hoe), and establish irrigation systems. Finally, in appreciation, Shun made Yu his successor on the Dragon Throne. In this capacity Yu solved more problems of both natural and supernatural origin, and laid the foundations of the administrative system which served China some four millennia by traditional reckoning.[9]

Mention might also be made of Plato's story of Atlantis, a land in the midst of the Atlantic, which was destroyed in a day and a night by volcanoes and then by the ocean waters that flooded over it. Plato may well have intended this account as one of his "myths" or teaching stories, for the point of his account seems to be comparing the tyrannical, militaristic civilization of the Atlanteans, who were invading the Mediterranean basin, with that of the nobler Athenians, who managed to check them. Presumably the destruction of Atlantis was due to the gods' displeasure, and so their island continent's submergence another example of a flood's purifying force. But the legend of Atlantis, which even if fictional could have been inspired by such actual events as the volcanic disaster that struck the Aegean island of Thera c. 1500 B.C.E., has taken on a life of its own, becoming a modern as well as an ancient myth.

Clearly, a flood serves as a kind of reprise and corrective of the initial creation, and of the original manifestations of evil. Its waters are like a return of the primal waters of chaos out of which the first creation emerged; water is at once destructive, cleansing, and renewing of life, even a token of rebirth, as in the Christian sacrament of baptism. At the same time, because the flood story comes after the first creation, perhaps even well after the "Next Generation," it recommends even more urgently that humanity must organize to correct its worst offenses, and keep itself in right relations with the divine.

So it is that myths of evil, like Pandora's Box, inevitably contain the element of hope.

CHAPTER 9

OUR PEOPLE: NATIONALISTIC MYTH

POLITICAL HISTORY AS RELIGIOUS HISTORY

John Gray, in his provocative work *Black Mass: Apocalyptic Religion and the Death of Utopia*, opens by saying, "Modern politics is a chapter in the history of religion." He goes on to explain, "The greatest of the revolutionary upheavals that have shaped so much of the history of the past two centuries were episodes in the history of faith – moments in the long dissolution of Christianity and the rise of modern political religion."[1]

Mythology has had its integral part in the long and often dismal, though also sometimes inspiring and hopeful, adventure of modern politics. That helps us to appreciate Gray's reminding us how much modern political movements have been religion under another name. The pseudo-religion label has frequently been applied to such causes as fascism and communism. They have certainly not hesitated to employ rhetoric, symbols, and rallies highly comparable to those of religion, and to demand a level of commitment like that of the strictest creeds.

These partisans have frequently taken older myths considered foundational to their states, and presented them in a manner suitable to present need. But we must also recognize that societies generally considered less ideological than those totalitarianisms have also subtly intertwined modern myths, or adaptations of ancient myths, with politics. One thinks of the role of the Arthurian myth in shaping the combined mystique of chivalry, the gentleman, and empire in Victorian and Edwardian England,[2] or of schoolbook versions of Plymouth Rock, George Washington, and the westward-moving frontier in the United States. To the latter we will return in a moment.

NATIONAL FOUNDATIONS

Before looking further at particularly modern permutations of national myth, we need to see how far back goes the association of foundational song and story with nationhood, or tribalism. For most societies ancient and modern have not only owned a mythic presentation of the origin of the world and of humanity in general, but also, at least by implication, of their own particular segment of it.

The Navajo Native Americans, for example, refer to themselves as the Diné, "the people," or the Diyin Diné, "the holy people," or "the people with supernatural power." Their elaborate myth of human origins, referred to earlier, in which they emerged from the ground, does not explicitly differentiate them from other peoples in that it does not assign to them a separate creation. Yet the complex Diné ceremonialism, such as the centrally important Blessingway rite, designed to maintain harmony with the universe, is based on the cosmogony of the Diné creation story. Other practices, such as the Enemyway ceremony, are mounted to counter the negative effects of contact with non-Diné people and their ghosts, so seem to assume that only some humans are "the people," or the people with the Diné's special supernatural power.[3]

Among the Australian Aboriginals, tribe, land, and ancestral totem were intimately related; one could hardly imagine one without the other. A particular people were those who knew how to recite a lengthy song associated with the tribal totem-ancestor – often a fairly obscure grub or lizard – who created that terrain, and for which his people have particular responsibility. He made land come to life back in the Dreamtime, by wandering about singing out the names of all that was to dwell therein, birds, animals, plants, rocks, waterholes, and spirit-wells, so calling them into being. Individual tribesmen today, by walking the same "songlines" and singing the same songs, with their narratives of what the totem ancestor did at each place for guidance, can walk the land and re-establish that primal connection: this is a profoundly meaningful act. Sometimes the same songline crosses the lands of several related peoples, changing language (but not melody, in which apparently are encoded landmarks and features of the land), as singers of today walkabout through the labyrinths of invisible pathways originating in the Dreaming that crisscross the Australia of its first inhabitants.[4]

A more explicitly particularizing story of national origins is that of ancient Israel. The biblical account tells us that, nine generations after Noah, God called out a descendant of Shem, one of the navigator's sons. This man, Abram, later called Abraham, dwelt in Mesopotamia. But God told him to leave that country and proceed with his family to a new land God would show him. He further said, "I will bless you and make your descendants into a great nation. You will become famous and be a blessing to others. I will bless anyone who blesses you, but I will put a curse on anyone who puts a curse on you. Everyone on earth will be blessed because of you" (Gen. 12:2–3).

Later, the relationship was formalized into a covenant or agreement between God, Abraham, and his descendant. When Moses received the divine law from God on Mount Sinai, it was clear this relationship involved not only blessing – significantly, the blessing was for all peoples through Abraham's people – but also grave responsibility, keeping a law which could be onerous, and which was not imposed on others. This story made it clear that the descendents of Abraham, later Hebrews, Israelites, or Jews, were different from others, and that the "fence of the law" helped them constantly to stay different because of special requirements regarding eating, marriage, and other ritual obligations.

A keynote of what has been called the national myth of the United States of America is the idea of that nation, whose early settlers knew the Bible well, as the "New Israel," with the events of its history correlated to those of ancient Israel. Thus the early settlers, especially the "Pilgrim Fathers" landing at Plymouth Rock, were like Abraham and his kin first coming into the Promised Land. George Washington leading that people into freedom from bondage to a foreign ruler is the American Moses,[5] whereas Abraham Lincoln, bringing liberation from slavery and reconciling brothers divided, dying at the hands of sinful men on Good Friday, was the American Christ.[6]

Another very famous ancient national story is the Aeneid, the great epic of the ancestors of Rome's founders by the poet Virgil.[7] A kind of Latin sequel to the popular Greek Iliad and Odyssey of Homer, it presents the story of Aeneas, a prince of Troy and a hero in the classic mold. He, after the fall of that doomed city, makes his way to Italy. His journey is inevitable because, the epic makes clear, fate has determined he will be the ultimate founder of mighty Rome.

Fate is decreed by Jupiter (the Greek Zeus, king of the gods), and Aeneas is befriended by Venus (Aphrodite) and Mercury (Hermes), even as he is opposed by Juno, Jupiter's wife, but in the Aeneid fate seems more powerful even than the gods. On the way Aeneas meets with many adventures, reminiscent of Odysseus's, culminated in his being shipwrecked in Africa where he meets Dido, Queen of Carthage, who falls deeply in love with him. But, reminded by Mercury of his inexorable fate, he reluctantly leaves Dido, who in her grief commits suicide. Like Odysseus, Aeneas then goes to the underworld, where he sees souls who will be reborn as famous Romans in the future, thus putting the narrative in the context of Rome's coming greatness. Arriving at Latium, an area ruled by King Latinus, he arranged, as fate decreed, to marry Lavinia, that ruler's daughter, but is opposed by other factions. The last half of the Aeneid, Virgil's Iliad, recounts the war that the hero had to wage before he successfully wed Lavinia and founded the city of Alba Longa.

Virgil's task was complicated by the fact that the fall of Troy was traditionally dated at 1184 B.C.E., and the founding of Rome at 743 B.C.E., and moreover that the Romans had their own legend that the city was founded by Romulus, who with his twin brother Remus had been suckled by a wolf. Virgil makes the boys' mother a descendant of Aeneas (their father was the god Mars), and so links the two stories: Aeneas is as it were father of the Roman people, Romulus the actual founder of the city.

The Aeneid was written in the time of Caesar Augustus, usually reckoned as the first and in many ways the greatest of the Roman emperors, under whom the empire showed promise of bringing the world to a new level of peace and prosperity. Many, including Virgil, believed, or at least hoped, this would be the case, and the epic was intended to express that vision. It was read in Roman schools, and has been basic to classical education down to the present. Indeed, which of what is popularly known of the Greco-Roman world really owes to the Aeneid; the famous story of the Trojan Horse, for example, is not actually found in the Iliad, but is best known from the Aeneid. The Aeneid, like the works of Homer, illustrate that it is the literary form of mythology which is usually most influential, above all in the political realm.

(Moving ahead to modern political myth, it is interesting to note that one of the few remnants of Mussolini's fascist rule one can see in Rome today are the long-lasting manhole covers, which in his campaign to recall modern Italians to their imperial legacy the dictator had imprinted with the emblem of Romulus and Remus at the she-wolf's teats, and the proud letters SPQR: *Senatus Populusque Romanus*, "The Senate and People of Rome," which had adorned the standards of the all-conquering legions of old. But, to the Duce's disappointment, modern Italian enthusiasm for re-enacting ancient victories was limited.)

MODERN POLITICAL MYTH

Political myth in the modern sense arose as a mixture of Enlightenment and Romantic influences. The eighteenth century brought the beginnings of scientific study of peoples and languages. A major advance was Sir William Jones's demonstration of the links between the Indo-European languages, a linguistic family extending from Sanskrit and its modern derivatives in India to most of the European tongues. Yet in his enthusiasm for all things Indo-European, Jones (who believed that Pythagoras and Plato must have been inspired by the "same fountain" as Vedanta) found it necessary, like many others soon to be caught up by the idea of a distinctively Indo-European, or "Aryan," language, culture, and putative race, to denigrate rival peoples, such as the Chinese or the Semitic, including the Jewish.[8] Since at the same time some of the European nations now proudly considering themselves Aryan were creating or maintaining colonial empires around the world, and seemed manifestly in advance of all others in every way, these beliefs were a convenient justification for their predominance. The Enlightenment ideal of the autonomous rational individual, of whom William Jones himself – broad-minded, politically liberal, friend of such luminaries as Samuel Johnson and Benjamin Franklin – was nearly a perfect exemplar, demanded as much, or so it seemed. For the Enlightenment (as well as for Christian missionaries), and for such nineteenth persons as the "Christian Socialist" Charles Kingsley or the philosopher John Stuart Mill, himself like Jones an employee of the East India Company, European expansionism was obviously an engine of progress and liberation for backward peoples imprisoned by too much myth and superstition.

But there was more. Indo-European myth was not only the voice of clear, bright minds; it was also Johann Herder's primal cry of a people "rooted" in their land and shaped by it in ways that echoes not only the voice of reason but also the powerful irrational forces newly exalted by romanticism. Myth in the modern "mythology" sense may have been discovered by the Age of Reason's nascent ability to look at languages and cultures, including their "myths," in a comparative, "scientific" way, the way we earlier spoke of as the Enlightenment mode. But "myth" did not stop there.

As the Enlightenment tide receded and that of Romanticism rolled in, the two combined with a growing European sense of nationhood, defined by language, culture, and even physical appearance, and expressed politically in Rousseau's notion of the "general will." In short, a nation was far more than boundaries on a map; it was an idea, a feeling, an identity, and – bring in myth – a story. Indeed, nationhood now demanded a story, even as Rome required the Aeneid, and whether unearthed or contrived, stories were found.

In the nineteenth century a romantic interest in folk culture and folklore swept across Europe, and elsewhere as well. From the Salvophiles of Russia to the "Celtic Twilight" (in the title of W. B. Yeat's book) mood in Ireland and the "Hindu Renaissance" in India, one found feeling-tinged praise of the virtue and simple wisdom of peasant life, and the profundity hidden beneath the unsophisticated wrappings of a nation's traditional folklore. This movement had both nationalistic and universalistic aspects, and could inspire both reform and reaction; it is too complex to be analyzed here. But it must be seen as a larger whole within which the nineteenth-century mythic revival, and the nationalism it inspired, can be placed, even as the more individualistic mid- to late-twentieth-century mythic revival can be seen in the context of the era's fascination with depth psychology.

One of the earliest lengthy constructions was Finland's Kalevala, composed by the poet Elias Lönrot in 1835 from many fragments of folklore to make for a vast narrative of heroic adventure and national identity. France's was the tale of Charlemagne, plus the French Revolution itself, and Napoleon. For Italy the story of the ancient Roman Empire, together with that of the nineteenth-century Risorgimento, was invaluable, especially as used by Italian fascists.

Germanic national myth begins with the battle of Teutonburg Forest in 9 C.E., when united Germanic tribes defeated three Roman

Legions, preventing their land from becoming part of the Roman Empire. The medieval *Nibelungenlied* may be based on folk memories of this event, together with much other history and folklore; it is best known now through the operas of Richard Wagner, and was much celebrated by nineteenth-century German nationalists wanting to bring their fragmented nation into unity like that of the ancient tribes n that heroic occasion. The fairy tales and folklore collected by the Brothers Grimm also helped creating a romantic concept of a Germanic nation founded on its *Volk* living close to the soil and their spiritual heritage.[9]

Enlightenment scholarship was ultimately based on the ideal of the autonomous rational individual, able to stand above his subject and analyze it dispassionately, just as the political ideal was an autonomous rational voter or, at the least, a well-advised enlightened monarch. Political and nationalistic Romanticism, on the other hand, essentially subordinated the individual to a larger unit such as the nation; one's highest moral fulfillment came through identification with the race, class, or nation's struggles and destiny. Twentieth-century fascism and communism both, broadly speaking, stem from that romantic vision together with some aspects, such as the idea of race, of Enlightenment thought. In fascism the larger group was the race or nation – "Aryan," Germanic; Germany, Italy – which then had to be defined against others, such as Slavs and "Semites." National myths could, and did, clearly play a large part in naming and energizing these identifications. As is well known, for German National Socialists, Nazis, the claim they were pure Aryans – Indo-Europeans – was central to their bizarre ideology.

For Marxists and Communists, the identification was with a social class, the workers, as well as with "progressive" intellectuals, and over against capitalism and imperialism. Once Russian communism took political power, identification was hardly less with a national entity, the Soviet Union. Useful myth quickly appeared, from accounts of earlier popular revolution to folklore seen as the voice of the oppressed.

An important link between mythology and the modern political myth is in the work of the French social scientist Georges Sorel (1847–1922).[10] An ambivalent figure, he began as a Marxist and became very interested in the political uses of myth and of revolutionary violence as redemptive and purifying, influencing among others Benito Mussolini. He held that heroic myths and the dramas of revolution were sources of social transformation, and so profoundly moral. The doctrines and "myths" behind them need not necessarily be true in some abstract sense, but are to be employed as tools of the insurrectionist's trade.

For Sorel, myths were apocalyptic "systems of images" able to inspire people battling for change to heroic struggle, and to envision coming victory. His "myths" were like soundbites and propaganda posters, less to be taken intellectually than as goads to feeling and action. Sorel was opposed to discursive thought and rationalistic thinking; for him what counted was revolutionary action against oppressors, getting the job done by whatever means necessary, and the triumphant images evoked by myth were weapons in that combat.

POLITICAL APOCALYPTIC MYTH

It is clear that political revolutionary ideologies and religious apocalyptic are not far apart on the deepest levels. Both envision a disastrous state of society prior; indeed, in which it seems evils are so rife they could hardly get worse. Then comes a dramatic breakthrough, whether from God or by grace of a preternaturally pure revolutionary elite, in which the situation is suddenly and unexpectedly reversed. The change comes in a way wonderful almost beyond telling, as though a new heaven and earth had descended. Movements like fascism and communism, as well as many religions, liked to talk about creating a "new man," as though sufficiently violent and all-consuming revolutionary activity, together with the environment of a new and radically different social order, like religious conversion, could thoroughly change one's whole character and personality.

The apocalyptic impact modern political myth can have, like the advent in power of a millenarian messiah, can hardly be better expressed than it was by Leni Riefenstahl, the great and controversial cinematographer, famous for her propaganda film on behalf of the German Third Reich, *Triumph of the Will*, documenting the 1934 Nazi rally in Nuremberg. Here she describes seeing Hitler at a rally she attended in late February 1932, less than a year before he came to power:

Hitler appeared, very late. The spectators jumped from their seats, shouting wildly for several minutes: "*Heil, Heil, Heil!*" I was too far away to see Hitler's face but, after the shouts died down, I heard his voice: "Fellow Germans!" That very same instant I had an almost apocalyptic vision that I was never able to forget. It seemed as if the earth's surface were spreading out in front of me, like a hemisphere that suddenly splits apart in the middle, spewing out an enormous jet of water, so powerful that it touched the sky and shook the earth. I felt quite paralyzed . . . New and unexpected thoughts shot through my mind.[11]

As another example from the same period of the nationalistic use of mythology, let us consider Japan before and during World War II, when the island nation was in the grip of extreme militaristic nationalists who sought to employ Shinto mythology to their ends. As we have seen, the basic Japanese myth tells us that the sun-goddess Amaterasu's grandson came down to earth to found the imperial line. However, in most periods of Japanese history the emperor, while a sort of sacred symbol, has had little real power compared to that of shoguns and other rulers.

But when in the late nineteenth century Japan acquired governments that wanted to bring the nation forceably into the modern world, they realized the authority of the emperor and the "imperial will" would greatly help legitimate the sacrifices required to create powerful industries and a world-class army and navy. Shinto was separated from the imported Buddhist faith to become a distinctive religion of the ancient Japanese kami, taught in schools and public lectures with special emphasis on the myth of imperial divine descent. One 1910 school textbook, invoking Confucian family values as well as Shinto imperialism, said:

It is only natural for children to love and respect their parents . . . . Our country is based on the family system. The whole country is one great family, and the Imperial House is the Head Family. It is with the feeling of filial love and respect for parents that we Japanese people express our reverence toward the Throne of an unbroken imperial line.[12]

By the 1930s, the period that, together with the war years, many Japanese call the "Dark Valley," the imperial mythos had become even more powerful. The *Kokutai no hongi*, or *Foundations of National Polity*, an important text issued by the Ministry of Education in 1937, declared that "Our country is established with the emperor, who is a descendant of Amaterasu Omikami [great kami], as her center, and our ancestors as well as we ourselves constantly have beheld in the emperor the fountainhead of her life and activities." Serving the emperor and his "great august will" was said to give life its rationale and was the source of morality, so that any deeds committed in accord with that will were unquestionably righteous, and not to be questioned. This is not, it was alleged, merely a matter of obedience, but more like a mystical loss of the self in something greater, "dying to self and returning to the One."[13] No less a figure than Hideki Tojo, both a general and prime minister of Japan for most of the war years, said, "It is only when I am exposed to the light of His Majesty that I shine."[14]

By 1945, however, most Japanese realized something was profoundly wrong in this mythologization of a modern nation's life and warlike activities. Japan, like most (though not all) modern countries, was willing to concede that nowadays myth may help individuals in their search for empowerment and identity, but nations are better guided by limited, pragmatic, and representative governments attuned to the pluralism of goals and beliefs of today's people, than by "one size fits all" ideologies.

POLITICAL MYTH TODAY

Do mythic images, stories "that tell us who we are," still influence political decisions? I was once with a group of students especially interested in myth, but when talk turned to politics, complaints were raised that too many people perversely vote against parties and policies one would think best represented the economic interests of their class and calling. Why was this? I responded that they, as students of myth, ought to know the answer better than most: people don't vote their pocketbook; they vote their myth. More money and benefits may sometimes seem less important than identifying with a leader or position that resonates with the stories and fantasies and ideal self-images one has within oneself; in America, those of the rugged, independent cowboy or pioneer, or of the victorious Second World War hero, still reverberate, as does all the power of ethnic and religious heritages. For others the Force lies in the epics of labor and civil rights struggles, or of idealized family life.

The point has often been made, and will be discussed further in the next chapter, that the comparison of political candidates is often as much or more a matter of comparative "images" than of actual ideas about public policy, and as visual media – television, the internet screen – gradually take the place of read material like newspapers and magazines for many people, "image" becomes only more important. Charisma: how a person looks, how one feels about his or her personality, whether this is a person about whom one would be enthusiastic as a leader, may well weigh as heavily, admit it or not, in deciding for whom to vote as policy positions. (And indeed, a case can be made that leadership ability, intangible as it may be, *is* important in a national leader.)

Another way of looking at the matter is to note that any candidate, or party, embodies a certain myth about the state, and this is inseparable from how one feels about his or her image or charisma. Of what myth about the history and meaning of the nation does this party and individual seem to be a part? And what kind of role in the myth does the person play? With questions like these, one can very often leverage a fascinating new perspective on the political processes going on all around, and perhaps better get an idea how best to be part of that process.

CHAPTER 10

THE WIZARD'S PRISM: THE PSYCHOLOGY OF MYTH

ANCIENT PSYCHOLOGY, MODERN PSYCHOLOGY

Psychology, like a prism held in the hand of a wizard, breaks the light of consciousness into its many colors and blendings. Mythology provides one chart against which to set that spectrum.

We might begin with a few words from James Hillman, a post-Jungian psychologist to be discussed a little later, on "the interchangeability of mythology and psychology." "Mythology," Hillman said, "is a psychology of antiquity. Psychology is a mythology of modernity."[1]

If psychology has any meaning for the understanding of myth, it would have to be that in some way myths help us think – about ourselves, what and who we are; about our relations to others, whether lovers, family, country, nation. Such no doubt did the common-coin myths of antiquity. (Myths do not necessarily make this kind of thinking easy. As we have seen, not a few mythic characters lead lives that are "over the top" and end in tragedy or despair, and many mythic families, including those involved in the original creation, are, in the contemporary term, dysfunctional to say the least. Yet the same could be said of current people and families as well, and somehow even the excesses of "heroes" can help us to see ourselves. I once met an individual who was dangerously suicidal; by reflecting deeply on two characters in that modern myth, *The Lord of the Rings*, Theoden and Denethor, likewise tempted by death, he realized he wanted to emulate Theoden, overcomer of despair's hold who rode on to honorable death, rather then Denethor, who gave in to the dark god and left only worse malaise in the ashes of his funeral pyre.)

Further, myths can show us *how* to think, at least in one way: the mythic way. Myth has roots in oral culture, before writing, and as we will see in a moment, that in itself may involve strikingly different ways of thinking, as well as communicating information, from the ways of the written word. The mythic manner of thinking is to think something through by telling a story about it: it can mean making even abstract or ideal images look and talk like characters in a story. As we have observed, our lives are stories, not abstractions; myth can make my life a meaningful story.

What does myth show us about the deepest roots of human thought? Roberts Avens, referring to Ernst Cassirer's theory of mythical thought, compares it to Plato's idea of knowing as recollection and Jung's discovery of archetypes: "Like Jung, Cassirer reverses the usual anthropomorphic nature of the mythical process. The primitive, instead of transferring his own finished personality (ego) to the god, first discovers himself as active spiritual principle through the figures of his gods; the human 'I' finds itself only through a detour in the divine 'I.' Avens cites the distinguished linguist Owen Barfield to the effect that early humankind does not animate (animism) a "dead world" with imagined souls and spirits, but rather the reverse: "It was not man who made the myths but myths or the archetypal substance they reveal, which made man."[2]

Even today, this way of going about figuring out problems and people may well be basic to thinking about our lives, our relationships, and our societies, insofar as our lives are themselves not generic abstractions but stories, albeit archetypal stories, stories that were there before we were. To be sure, we are not simply a worker, a mother, a student; a good person or a bad person; but a real individual with a unique story special to ourselves behind all these roles. Yet we can feel lost without stories larger and older than ourselves to go with those roles. A person trying to decide between two men or women for a long-term relationship may find himself or herself fantasizing a sort of story about what life with each would be like; balancing between two possible jobs, the individual may visualize a story-like scenario to go with each. And, if the situation is new to us personally, the stories will have come from somewhere else: observation, reading, cinema, whatever; but in the end we may find that, in their profoundest essence, they are as old as myth itself.

127

BOUNDARIES AND LIMITS

similar to stories, myths...

Yet there are limits to mythic story-thinking as well. As stories, myths have to have a plot, and any plot involves a protagonist with whom the reader or hearer identifies, and obstacles, usually personified by an antagonist, that must be defeated and overcome. So far, so good. We all have an identity, and we all have problems and barriers to conquer; a good heroic story can be an inspiration as we confront those challenges.

basic

But myths can easily make the hero and the enemy far more black-and-white than they are likely to be in ordinary real life; they can encourage in us what the Jungians would call "inflation" with the all-competent hero, mother, lovely maiden, or whatever our archetype is, and reduce the adversary to the "Shadow." Real life usually calls for more complex characters than this, and a more nuanced view of good guys and bad guys, since we probably all have something of both in ourselves. Do the boundaries we want to set up between our group and another – our country, our religion, our culture – really stand up when tested against our common humanity?

are there boundaries with myths

And do even the boundaries, with their myths, that distinguish our species from others hold against feelings obviously common to all sentient beings? Sometimes myths give another perspective when they make animals talk and act as nobly, or more nobly, than humans.

THE WORLD OF MYTH AND ITS CHARACTER-PARTS

Myth, then, can tell us more about how we think than is apparent at first glance, if we are prepared to engage the world of myth both appreciatively and critically. The range of character-types in myths may seem limited: for men, the good or bad hunter, warrior, king, or magician; for women, the maiden, mother, crone – or evil enchantress. Many may seem to be stereotyped, especially before later literary versions of the tale appear. Is this helpful, by giving us an ideal, or dangerous, by over-simplifying reality?

The psychology of myth has other aspects as well. No doubt, as many psychological commentators would assert, the nature of gods and heroes may express our deep innermost feelings, both acknowledged and unacknowledged. The parricide in Greek and other myths, the amoral exploits of Coyote, the omnipotent child that was Krishna, the maidens who are nothing but seductive sorceresses, the warriors for whom winning, with its "honor" and "glory," is every-thing – all these and more may represent impulses we know are there, whether that is who, in our rational mind, we really want to be or not. They can help us identify and name these parts: that's my trick-ster, or my Calypso.

what myth illustrates

Likewise, in regard to the universe as a whole, myths illustrate how cosmos, like lives, contains both order and disorder: the stars turn like clockwork, yet here below the unexpected, including disaster and death, is a frequent visitor. Myths also demonstrate the range of ways humans can respond to the mystery, and the many moods we impose upon ourselves as we do so. We treat death and disaster as comedy or as inexorable tragedy, as whimsy to be laughed off or as evil to the fought, or in terms of gaining recompense in another life.

myths allow us to escape

Another psychological function of myth is that it offers alterna-tive worlds of wonder, places of escape and refreshment from this one. Especially for those lonely or oppressed, stories set in realms of beauty and marvel cast as on a silver screen rainbow counterpoints to drab outer reality. While no doubt compensation can go too far, so that people live largely in fantasy and fail to face their problems honestly, certainly nothing is wrong with some stretching of mind and imagination even when outwardly in narrow quarters.

HOW IS MYTH BELIEVED?

In what way are myths understood in traditional societies, especially those tales that appear to present a simply absurdist world: talking animals, return from death? For myself, I believe that traditional and archaic peoples knew the difference between mythic and everyday reality, between what is said to have happened "back then" and what happened yesterday in the course of everyday life. They did not nec-essarily "believe" their myths in the same way fundamentalists, for example, say one ought to believe scriptures.

What "belief" means in much of modern religion really developed together with the emergence of modern science, especially in the eighteenth century and after. Conservative "belief" now insists that a religious teaching, say the story of creation in the Book of Genesis, ought to be accepted as literally, factually true in the same way a sci-entist would take the distance of the earth from the sun, or say that water is composed of hydrogen and oxygen – or that creation began with the "big bang." But that is truth in modern science, not traditional religion. Traditional religionists, of course, affirmed the myth, insofar as they had no alternative explanation. But the details were not important points of contention; like all stories, they could be told in many different ways; compare the first two chapters of Genesis, or the many Greek or Hindu myths of origins. What was important was the way myth opened up into a world of wonder, of a sense of invisible as well as visible powers all around best accessed through narrative; theirs was not the fundamentalist state of mind which holds that religious truth must be on a par with scientific.

FREUDIAN MYTHOLOGY

We may now look at a few important modern psychological perspectives on myth, starting with Sigmund Freud. We have already outlined Freud's basic position, and that need not be repeated here. We might look instead at his application, and for that we turn to the Preface of Joseph Campbell's first major work, *The Hero with a Thousand Faces*. Campbell is often thought of as more Jungian than Freudian, but in fact the Freudian influence, especially in his earlier work, written in the 1940s and 1950s heyday of Freudian cultural influence, is hardly less important as background. The author commences by quoting Freud's *The Future of an Illusion* (the illusion being religion): "The truths contained in religious doctrines are after all so distorted and systematically disguised, that the mass of humanity cannot recognize them as truth"; Campbell then proceeds to say, "It is the purpose of the present book to uncover some of the truths disguised for us under the figures of religion and mythology by bringing together a multitude of not-too-difficult examples and letting the ancient meaning become apparent of itself."[3]

For Campbell, as for Freud and his disciple Géza Róheim, who greatly influenced Campbell, these meanings are essentially those uncovered by psychoanalysis: the child's relationship to his then-gigantic and omnipotent parents, and his discovery of his body and himself. For example, Campbell discussed the familiar Hansel-and-Gretel type of story of the evil witch who lives in a candy house that seems good to eat, but actually she wants to eat the children. In the end, however, the children outsmart her. This, we are told, represents the infant's dual image of the mother: at once, through the breast, something good to eat, yet at the same time causing deep anxiety over her possible absence, or her anger, leading to fantasies of

danger, separation, and disaster. Those fears are only enhanced by
the Oedipal factor so crucial to Freud: the half-conscious desire of
the boy to kill the father and have the mother to himself, accompanied by dread of punishing castration by the father, who becomes a
fearsome ogre; and the corresponding Electra complex of the girl, as
rival of the mother for the father's love, "living in fear that the ogress
may kill him and draw herself back into the web of the nightmare of
that presexual cannibal feast (formerly paradise!) [of] the bambino
and madonna."[4]

It remains to be added that many have seen Freud himself as less
a scientist in the strict sense than a myth-maker, or even a visionary
poet. If his categories like id, ego, and super-go, his myth-based
Oedipal Complex and his theory of the beginning of religion in the
killing of a primal father, are taken not as absolutely and objectively
true in the sense that water is composed of hydrogen and oxygen, but
as actors in a myth that is true in the sense all great novels or poems
– or religious mythologies – are true, one can see his controversial
theories in a new light. James Hillman quotes Adolf Guggenbühl-
Craig to the effect that, "The Freudians cannot properly understand
Freud because they take him at his word. The Jungians may be better
at understanding Freud because they can read him for his mythology."[5]

JUNGIAN MYTHOLOGY

Jung's position has been outlined. Let us look at another myth in
Jungian terms. Jung's disciple Maria-Louise von Franz presents a
story from Grimm's fairy tales of a woman who had a daughter and
a step-daughter. One day God appeared to them as a poor man and
asked directions to the village. The woman and her daughter scorned
him, but the step-daughter showed the way, and for that was given
three gifts: great beauty, immense wealth, and the kingdom of
heaven when she died. But the other two were made exceedingly ugly.
After many events, in which the woman tried to punish her much-
favored step-daughter every way she could, through the help of the
step-daughter's brother, Reginer, who is the king's coachman, the
beauty succeeded in marrying the king.

Von Franz begins in a typical Jungian way to regard the three
women as a triad representing the feminine psyche: the mother the
conscious attitude, the unworthy daughter the negative shadow, the

step-daughter the true inner nature and power of renewal within the feminine psyche. Reginer, as the animus or male aspect of the psyche, is the hero-guide, and the king is the discerning logos or reasoning principle, with whom connection must be made for full renewal and eternal life.[6]

ARCHETYPAL PSYCHOLOGY

A disciple of Jung's who has gone his own way is Hillman, developer of "archetypal psychology."[7] He distinguishes his position from that of Jung by asserting that, whereas Jung focused on the self and its constituent parts – ego, anima, animus, shadow, together with the archetypes, and wanting to unify this constellation into a mandala around the individuated self, his is a "polytheistic psychology", which recognizes and accepts the innumerable myths and fantasies (visualized as gods, goddesses, heroes, people, and animals) that fashion our inner lives, and express themselves in the many dreams we have and roles we play.

Hillman's human consciousness is a labyrinthine cave of images, with neither beginning nor end, though the light may shift from one picture to another. The archetypalist wants to set up no one constricting ego into which everything has to be pushed, or one monistic unified self that, as "hero" or "imperial ego," should "ascend" at the cost of not fulfilling its polytheistic potential for multiplicity and diversity. Wholeness, for Hillman, is instead a self at home with a multiplicity of imaginal representation, each received with joy in its own time, a polytheistic sequence of many gods.

Needless to say, Hillman is skeptical of the notion of spiritual growth, which he sees as merely a fixation on the maturation process of childhood and youth. But true adulthood is not progressing "to" anything. It is rather the capacity to enjoy the infinitely varied experiences that life has to offer. Such a personality is not an ego or self, in what Hillman sees as the restrictive sense; nor is it a "spirit" made only for dwelling on the level of exalted experiences. It is rather a "soul," a term having to do with the "inside meaning" of human experience, embraced by such terms as heart, life, warmth, humanness, suffering, loss, innocence, sinful, and what is implied when one says eyes are "soulful."

Obviously, such an outlook would be capable of very rich interaction indeed with myth, seen as models of soul-making psychological polytheism: here are gods and heroes to mirror our inner deities of love and striving, making and unmaking, wisdom and vanity; of this hearth and home and that distant mountain, this ocean and that constellation above. Hillman particularly loves Greek mythic figures, and has used them widely in his work. For example, in *The Dream and the Underworld*, after citing the pre-Socratic philosopher Heraclitus, with whom he understandably feels much kinship, to the effect that "You could not find the ends of the soul though you traveled every way, so deep is its logos [meaning]," he tells us that Hades, the Underworld, "was of course the God of depths, the God of invisibles." He has no altars and no family on earth, save for a shadowy connection with his brother Zeus, ruler of the upper world of light as he is of the lower world of dark. His main relationship to our world is through seizure, as in his taking of Persephone; otherwise, he is that which timeless, unseen, dark, deep beyond all imagining, which stands always over against our brief hours in the sun.[8]

The work of Roberts Avens might be said to take Hillman even farther.[9] Avens brought together the thought of the great Islamicist Henry Corbin and the latter's interpretation of the Sufi philosopher Ibn 'Arabi, who posited an "imaginal" realm ("realm of images") between ordinary individual consciousness and the One. This is the level represented by the archetypes of all religions, the angels, gods, buddhas, and immortals, together with the figures of myth and dream.

The point is that this level of reality is absolutely real, as real as God and groundhogs, as trees and trumpets, as you and me. It is just not physical – nor is it pure spirit, like God – so it cannot be touched or weighed, but it affects us, interacts with us nonetheless, in its own way. The imaginal is not just imaginary, not just a projection of our own thoughts alone, for it has much in common across the human world; yet it is within us too, as the basis of that endless hall of images. It is the homeland of myth.

Something like this was also what Friedrich Schelling, in his lectures on mythology, apparently meant by "potencies" (*potenzen*) which underlie myth.[10] Like the archetypal psychologists, he rejected any simplistic idea that mythic beings are only psychological projections of the mind, because he believed that they represent realities that can only be told in myth, in story-form; they are not merely codes or allegories for something else more "modern" and abstract.

He also did not literally believe in the many gods of traditional mythology. Yet those gods are what he called "potencies," forces, one might say, on the interface between individual consciousness and divine consciousness, which take innumerable mythical forms, but which are themselves still there if the forms are stripped away, for they are not identical with any of them. One could say they are aspects of God, but only if one recognizes with Schelling that God contains within himself not only the individual consciousness, but also the rational and non-rational, God and "not-God," in eternal interaction. This seems very much like the imaginal realm, wherein are played out the dramas of myth.

Incidentally, well before Hillman and Avens (though not Schelling) the philosophical novelist Aldous Huxley had vividly put forward a similar notion of almost infinite realms within mind, in his case in age-of-exploration language of seas and continents and their strange fauna:

> If I have made use of geographical and zoological metaphors, it is . . . because such metaphors express very forcibly the essential otherness of the mind's far continents, the complete autonomy and self-sufficiency of their inhabitants. A man consists of what I may call an Old World of personal consciousness and, beyond a dividing sea, a series of New Worlds – the not too distant Virginias and Carolinas of the personal subconscious and the vegetative soul; the Far West of the collective unconscious, with its flora of symbols, its tribes of aboriginal archetypes; and across another, vaster ocean, at the antipodes of everyday consciousness, the world of Visionary Experience.[11]

The motif of exploration, rather than of knowing the gods, evoked by this passage is of course no less mythological than Hillman's Greek gods. Indeed, exploration is one of the great themes of myth: Bran the Blessed, Jason in search of the Golden Fleece, the quest for the Grail Castle or Shambhala. Either way, there are many worlds and wonders within one, and myth is a royal road to their discovery.

ORAL THINKING

Here is a perspective from another wing of psychology, the behavioral and neurological. A book by Maryanne Wolf, *Proust and the Squid*, discusses the differences between oral and literate communication, and the ways of thinking that lie behind the two.[12] (The odd title comes from a line from the great French novelist Marcel Proust, when he described reading as "that fruitful miracle of a communication in the midst of solitude," and the requirements of bioneurological research, in which the optic nerves of squid, a hundred times larger than the mammalian, are far more accessible for study.)

The first point made is that reading is really an unnatural activity for humans, developed far too recently for neurological evolution to code for it. We read only because the brain was able to re-adapt circuitry originally intended for other purposes, such as distinguishing two kinds of plants rather than two kinds of letters. It is worth noting too that it has only been within the last 150 years or so that reading became truly widespread even in "civilized" countries; until then it was the province of an elite "reading class," and naturally the information, and the culture, encoded in letters was one support of their privilege and power.

Do really significant differences lie between ways of understanding and assimilating, even between ways of thinking, in oral and literate cultures? This question is crucially important for the study of myth, since surviving myths and folktales are by far our most significant legacy from oral culture before writing came along – even though we now tend to know them through written records.

A study by Aleksandr R. Luria, a Soviet psychologist, based on 1930s interviews with illiterate and newly literate peasants in Uzbekistan and Kyrgyzstan found that between them differences did indeed exist.[13] Illiterates expressed ideas through graphic images, and in story form, while literates were far more comfortable than they with abstract categories and hypothetical situations. For example, literate people used generic color terms like "dark blue" or "light yellow," but illiterates used metaphors like "liver," "peach," or "cotton in bloom" to describe colors. In another experiment, illiterates were shown a picture containing a hammer, a saw, an axe, and a log, and were asked to name the three that were similar.

The non-readers said they were all useful. If pressed, they would exclude the hammer, on the grounds it could not be used to cut the log like the saw or axe. Clearly, they were not thinking in terms of generic categories, but in terms of the beginning of a story – doing something with the objects, cutting wood.

When told that some viewers had grouped the three tools together, excluding the log, they laughed, saying "That person must have enough firewood already." When shown a picture of three adults and a child and asked which one of those didn't fit, they refused to exclude the child, saying he needed the adults and they needed the child to run errands – again, the picture immediately becomes not a puzzle but a story – thinking by means of story-telling.

For non-literate oral culture, then, understanding immediately becomes an exercise in story rather than abstract logic. Orals store their thoughts in stories. There is more: as another student of orality and reading, Walter J. Ong, has pointed out, to be memorable, and so remembered, a story needs protagonists and opponents, us and them. It calls for conflict, and violent and passionate events, to summon up the "juices" that energize good memorization – the tale must become myth, not mere chronicle.[14] Moreover, unlike the printed page, oral story-telling values repetition and stereotype; they represent accumulated wisdom to be passed on. Nor is borrowing from others plagiarism; using another's words is keeping alive lore handed down through many mouths. But the critic's questioning analysis is ill-favored, for weighing words risks putting priceless traditional wisdom in jeopardy.

At the same time, since no written record lies archived of how a story was told in the past, the way the tale is told now is simply the way it is; an oral narration has in effect no earlier version, nor inconsistencies to be reconciled, that would ordinarily concern today's audience. Such issues, according to Ong, would usually be noted only after it has been put down on paper. By the same token, mythic times are always in the same undated past equally far removed from the present.

A story needs a story-teller. The classicist Eric A. Havelock noted that Plato, who was literate, seemed uneasy about the effort it took an actor or bard to memorize the vast amounts of oral material his craft required. This labor meant virtual identification with the part or the story, almost like being in trance or enchantment by the tale, so that objectivity, even one's own separate identity, was lost. Reciting or acting was like entering a dream, which for Plato was not a positive state, but rather like that of those prisoners in the *Republic* who were lost in the illusion of seeing only the shadows of reality, forgetting their own true nature.[15] (This state is not unknown to actors even today, who can sometimes be observed playing their main characters off stage or screen as well as on.)

So it is that bardic or theatrical presentation of an essential story had – and still has – a force quite different from reading it in a book, or even hearing it read aloud in a flat, objective manner. It meant entering a trance or dream along with the performer. Think of a distinction between intense and passive communication. Much of what we read we take in passively, but to listen to the words of an individual – especially one who is on fire with a message – in person, or even on screen, is more likely to be an intense experience, so much so it can cause either passionate commitment to the message, or visceral reaction against it. Many of us can read, even with amusement, the words of a political or religious figure with whom we disagree, but find it highly unpleasant to have to listen to the same ideologue directly.

The point is that in oral culture, messages are not only told in story form, but also are more likely to come at us in intense form. They demand visceral response, if they are not merely entertainment, and where there is no alternative narrative, that response would undoubtedly be in favor of the worldview and implied course of action of the story. We would be ready, indeed eager, for festival, hunting, sacrifice, even war. The effect would be to reinforce a society's worldview and self-image.

The observation remains to be made, as it was earlier proposed by Wolf, Ong, and others, that our contemporary culture seems to be drifting slowly back toward the mythic, intense media world of spoken communication. In our brave new post-modern world, oral communication seems to be surging as reading declines. Today, more and more people get the communications that really matter to them in story form, on the movie and television screen, or the internet monitor – especially as even there, the YouTube model of instant story interpreting anything looks to be gradually to be overtaking the Wikipedia model of cool literate information at one's fingertips.

What kind of world would this trend, if continued, produce? Perhaps one even more deeply divided than now along political and religious lines, as people listen to "hot" speakers with whom they resonate, whether politicians or preachers, and shun those to whom the response to too grueling to be endured. On the other hand, the internet is said to make for a new democracy of incredible diversity, a world of countless stories told by the humble as well as the great, even each may be limited to the six or eight minutes of a YouTube flick. That would call forth a planet of countless myths with real personalities behind them, and in back of those thronging souls the archetypes of Jung and the endless dream-caverns of Hillman, from which myths emerge, and where perhaps anything can happen. What do you think?

CHAPTER 11

THE THINKERS: NOTABLE SCHOLARS AND PHILOSOPHERS OF MYTH

Here are a few representative figures in the development of mythology since the late eighteenth century, when the modern study of myth took shape. The new mythology arrived in the wake of Sir William Jones and the discovery of the Indo-European language family. It was also abetted by collections of European folklore made in the nineteenth century by researchers like the Grimm Brothers in Germany, or Lady Gregory and Lady Wilde in Ireland.

(Some important individuals who have been presented previously, such as Claude Lévi-Strauss under "Theories of Myth" or Sigmund Freud, Carl Jung, and James Hillman under "Myth and Psychology," will not be described again in this chapter. In a few cases, however, an account with a different emphasis will be offered here.)

JOHANN GOTTFRIED VON HERDER (1744–1803)

Herder was a particular important figure in the age of the Enlightenment as it morphed into Romanticism. His "Volkish" school of mythology emphasized the close identity of myth with the "Volk" – people, country, or ethnicity, especially seen in light of their presumptively original rural roots and nearness to native land and soil. Herder speculated that once a single people dwelt with one language in an original "Garden of Eden," but then, in a development like that of the biblical story of the Tower of Babel, they were dispersed into many nations and tongues across the face of the earth. In their new homelands, however, each found rootedness in its own soil, and told stories to go with the union of land and people.

Herder stressed the close interplay between language and myth – indeed, myth was an original form of language – and the natural environment of its people. Like many romantics of his age, he was appalled by the crass, dehumanizing aspects of the industrial revolution springing up all around. Like them, he harbored a nostalgic image of traditional rural life. Believing country people to have a noble simplicity and clarity of vision lost by city dwellers, he held up their myths and stories as examples of the primal vision and pristine nature of the race.[1]

Herder also lived in a period of accelerating nationalism in Europe, when lands and peoples, above all those fragmented or under the thumb of larger empires, were eager to seize on tokens of distinctive identity and noble heritage. The reconstruction of "national myths" was a significant part of this process. Nowhere was this more the case than in his own Germany, broken up into numerous small kingdoms, duchies, and principalities, or else, during the Napoleonic wars, under hated French domination. "Volkish" thinkers and propagandists quickly seized on Herder's ideas to construct an ideal German nationality far older and deeper than the petty divisions, and yearning to realize itself.

Herder can hardly be blamed retroactively for the evils to which German Volkish nationalism was ultimately to lead. He did not mean to imply that the national mythology of one country was better than that of another, just different; and so much was the "national" idea in the air at his time, it can hardly all the attributed to one source. Nonetheless, Herder's work again reminds us that mythological thought can rarely be separated from the biases and "needs," consciously acknowledged or not, of its age. In a real sense, though, that observation simply reflects the nature of myths themselves, which presumably from their earliest human beginnings were stories told in response to the yearnings and wisdom-requirements of peoples and, as in the case of all drama and recitation, how they were understood was a co-creation of performer and audience.

FRIEDRICH WILHELM JOSEPH VON SCHELLING (1775–1854)

Schelling was the philosopher in the German idealist tradition most interested in mythology, a topic on which he gave a series of published lectures.[2] He was a major precursor of Freud and the psychoanalysts in understanding the unconscious. His work is too rich and varied to be summarized in a few phrases. We have noted, however, that he looked at myth in terms of "potencies," which, like Jungian archetypes of the unconscious, express in ways colored by the cultural environment presences deep in consciousness that are, nonetheless, more universal than the single individual. So far as the background of this mythological thought is concerned, we could compare it to Schelling's view of art which, he asserted, is not merely the self-expression of individual artists – indeed, the artist does not fully understand his own work – but is beauty *as* the realization of the Infinite in the Finite. Nature itself is, in this sense, a divine work of art. On the human plane, myth, like all art, stands at a triple interface between individual poet, universal human, and the Infinite.

Schelling's place in the history of mythological thought lies in the way his relating of mythology and romanticism pointed in a different direction from the Volkish world of Herder and nationalism, Schelling's vision, incorporating the romantics' exaltation of imagination and aesthetics (the creation and appreciation of art) into understanding myth, explored realms of mind later to be called the unconscious. With the help of myth, he pioneered terrain later charted by twentieth-century psychoanalysis, and by perceiving the deep wells of the unconscious to be one fountainhead of myth, he prepared the way for the new individualistic mythology of the that century.

FRIEDRICH NIETZSCHE (1844–1900)

The enigmatic philosopher Nietzsche influenced mythology significantly, although as we have noted before, this influence is not easy to define precisely. One thinks of his sometime close association with Richard Wagner, creator of a Germanic operatic myth-cycle; his contributions to mythology through his distinction between the Apollonian and Dionysian – rational and ecstatic – styles; and his formulation of his own new myth in Zarathustra, proclaimer of the Death of God. Cristiano Grottanelli has also pointed out that, in *The Birth of Tragedy*, Nietzsche portrayed the suffering of Prometheus as illustrating the profound idea "that humanity's highest goal must be bought with crime and suffering," and suggesting that myth is the appropriate vehicle for the revelation of such terrible truths, perhaps too horrible to be perceived directly.[3]

Indeed, in *Thus Spake Zarathustra*, he had that original proclaimer of monotheism now declare that God is dead, and we have killed him. The German thinker thereby showed, as well as taught, that myth must be created anew *today*, for only myth is capable of bearing the overwhelmingly painful, powerful, and liberating reality of *our* world: that God is dead, and we ourselves have murdered him.

(This last statement could only be made in a mythological sense. Nietzsche, and the "Death of God" theologians of the 1960s, insisted that the Death of God was not to be taken in a merely metaphorical sense, to mean that we have lost faith in God, or that there never was any God but we didn't realize it until now. Yet on the other hand, gods do not just die, at least in the nineteenth, twentieth, and twenty-first centuries. The Death of God must mean something neither untrue nor true, but that happened in a special mythological realm. What do you think?)

SIR JAMES GEORGE FRAZER (1854–1941)

Frazer was a monumental figure in his generation, talked about on Main Street as well as in ivied halls. His great work *The Golden Bough* (1890–1918), eventually running to some 12 weighty volumes in various editions and enlargements, was influential not only in anthropology and mythological studies, but also in literature, drama, psychology (including Freud), and the way many people thought when it came to myth and religion, especially primitive.[4]

Frazer was not a field anthropologist. Scottish-born, he traveled little and spent most of his uneventful adulthood as a scholarly Cambridge University professor; it has been said that his biography is essentially a list of books. But the world, often at its most primitive and grotesque, came to *him* instead. In his study at Cambridge, Frazer collected and sorted voluminous accounts of myth and ritual sent in by missionaries and colonial officials from around the world. These he combined with classical sources to produce a distinctive theory of myth.

For Frazer, the touchstone was sacred kingship. Around the archaic world, he thought, the well-being of the king and the land were bound up together. When a ruler's power began to wane, he needed to be sacrificed for the good of the tribe, or killed and superseded by another aspirant for highest office.

The Golden Bough commences with a dramatic account from the sacred grove of Diana of the Wood at Nemi, near Rome. A legend going back to ancient times says that if a runaway slave was successful in pulling down a bough from a special golden tree, he then won the right to fight the priest of that shrine to the death, and if successful to succeed him as priest and "King of the Wood." Dramatically Frazer describes the wariness of the priest by day, and well into the night, as he keeps an eye out for such a dangerous visitor, and we are then off into many pages and finally volumes of archaic lore in this vein.

Several other seminal ideas, such as views of totemism and the concept of the scapegoat (which influenced Robert Girard), emerged from Frazer's immense body of writing as well. Frazer also developed a theory of the evolution of thought from magic to religion and finally to science. His distinction between magic and religion was influential: magic is the attempt to *control* nature and events through occult power; religion is instead *asking* spiritual beings for help.

Frazer's view of sacred kingship has not been borne out by subsequent research, and in general his work is regarded as outdated. *The Golden Bough* and other works remain, however, an absorbing collection of myth and ritual from around the world. Frazer painted a colorful panorama of myth and ritual from the farthest and wildest extremes of earthly space and time, together with provocative if not always convincing theoretical interpretations, and made it available to the reading public. Not a few myth students who later moved on to more sophisticated views were first attracted to the fascination of comparative mythology on opening the pages of *The Golden Bough*.[5]

ERNST CASSIRER (1874–1945)

The German-Jewish philosopher Cassirer was best known for his work on symbolism. His *Philosophy of Symbolic Forms* appeared in three volumes from 1923 to 1929; the second was *Language and Myth*.[6] Cassirer emphasized that language and myth developed in tandem with each other, both representing important sides of human consciousness. Language, through its grammar and symbolic nature, bears within itself the power of logic and abstract thought; it developed into mathematics and science. Myth, on the other hand, leads to art, poetry, and visionary insight. Both language and myth are human constructs, but mighty in their ability to stimulate creativity. They help us express our experience and, in the expression, make the experience itself more profound. Seeing the full moon can be a splendid vision. But talking about the moon scientifically, and on the other hand writing a poem or painting a picture celebrating the Queen of Night, each opens up very different human capacities.

Cassirer was convinced that both science and what he meant by myth need to progress together. Too much of modern life has taken the language side as what is serious and really important, regarding the myth side as entertaining, perhaps even high culture, but finally less weighty than language, perhaps a matter of individual taste. But that attitude has depleted humanity. It leads ultimately to a robot-like existence.

At the same time, as one who experienced Nazi Germany before going into exile, Cassirer was well aware of what can happen when a nation falls victim to myth. When myth turns demonic, the rational language side of consciousness is desperately needed to counteract it. It is also important that the raw power of primal myth be tempered through its artistic and poetic expression. For myth, important as it is, to be brought into cultivated and civilized life, it must be tamed, refined into high art and poetry. Perhaps Ovid's skeptical, urbane renditions of old myths are an example, and the great "pagan" art of the Renaissance another.

This does not mean that myth has to be assigned a meaning, in the naive sense of those who see merely allegory, or veiled metaphysics, or even the acting-out of psychological dynamics in myth. Myth is something more than this, though that "more" is hard to express, because "Myth is nontheoretical in its very meaning and essence. It defies and challenges our fundamental categories of thought." It has, Cassirer concludes, both conceptual and perceptual structures; it is a way of seeing as well as a way of thinking, both different from the modern, but no less real, "for every feature of our human experience has a claim to reality."[7]

Cassirer emphasized the relation of myth to ritual and dramatic performance; ritual is simply organizing the body, along with space, time, and objects, to enact a cosmological or mythical event. What does this mean to the ritualist or actor? Originally, he held, the participant with a mask simply *was* the divine figure portrayed. Later, Cassirer said, primal myth-drama became religion when a *distinction* between human rite and its transcendent referent was perceived. However, that distinction may still remain tenuous in some enduring sacred rites, as when the shaman in trance *becomes* the deity possessing him.

The American philosopher Susanne Langer (1895–1985) was a disciple and translator of Cassirer. Her accessible works, particularly *Philosophy in a New Key* (1942), both popularized Cassirer and presented her own interesting philosophy of art and drama. Her ideas of why drama is important have reverberation for mythology. Myth after all was originally bardic or dramatic performance, and arguably is still best appreciated as drama or, today, as cinema. Langer contended that drama creates a kind of "virtual history," which causes us to see each moment of action as growing out of its antecedents and leading to its inevitable fulfillment, as though guided by Destiny; we see life as history in action.

In myth, too, one feels that important sense of actions larger than themselves in significance, because they are rooted in the past and leading toward an End; even the freedom of individual characters is somehow part of that larger meaning. Indeed, the ability to induce that feeling may be a defining characteristic of myth, as over against other stories. Myth, Langer said, does not stem from a "religious feeling," either of dread or of mystic veneration, but from inner life, beginning with private dreams and fantasies, externalized and made public.[8] While such a view may be too limited, it does no doubt hone in on the unknown bards of the beginning who were the very first to give voice to myths that, forming first deep in their own minds, ultimately became communal tradition.

GEORGES DUMÉZIL (1898–1986)

The French scholar Georges Dumézil, best known for his comparative study of Indo-European mythology, began as a follower of Frazer and *The Golden Bough*, but ultimately came to believe its basic theory, that myth and ritual everywhere are based on the killing and replacement of kings or heroes as their power fades, was too limited. As though in substitution for that focus, by 1938 he had discovered another theme at least of Indo-European myth: the tripartite division of society, and the gods, into three classes or "functions." Reflected well in the three "twice-born" castes of India, *brahmins*, *kshatriyas*, and *vaisyas*, these are priests, rulers/warriors, and craftsmen/workers. Under the influence of the great sociologist of religion Émile Durkheim, Dumézil was clear that major social realities are "collectively represented" in heaven, and in myth. Thus the three castes of India just mentioned were, he believed, shown in the Vedic pantheon as Varuna and Mitra (first function), Indra (second function), and the Asvins or Divine Horsemen (third function).

In the ancient Vedas, Varuna and Mitra were high gods whose main task was upholding *rta* or cosmic law. Indra, the most popular deity, prototype of the Indo-European warrior like Thor, dwelt in the atmosphere and wielded lightning; he thundered across the sky in a chariot accompanied by a boisterous band of warrior-companions called Maruts. The twin Asvin brothers also rode chariots through the heavens, but they were portrayed as benign, and concerned with the fertility of flocks, fields, and families.

The same pattern spread across the Indo-European world, being no less displayed in Greek, Roman, Germanic, and Celtic myth and society. In the Old Norse world, for example, Odin is first function, Thor second, and Freyr, the god of fertility and hence of farming people, the third.

Dumézil's thesis has inevitably produced scholarly debate, many feeling that while there may be some truth to it in some instances, superimposing it as the interpretive key on a whole range of mythology has sometimes been forced. Nonetheless, as is so often the case, the presence of such a schematic, when supported by scholarship as capable as that of Dumézil, has been a powerful impetus for further important work.[9]

MIRCEA ELIADE (1907–86)

Born in Romania, Mircea Eliade attended the University of Bucharest, He was able to spend 1928 to 1931 studying Indian philosophy and yoga in India, afterwards finishing his doctorate. (One of his best-known books, *Yoga: Immortality and Freedom* [1958] is a considerably enhanced later version of his dissertation.) He became a professor at the University of Bucharest, where he spent the 1930s, popular not only as a young university lecturer, but also as a journalist and novelist. It was during the later 1930s that the youthful celebrity supported the Legion of the Archangel Michael, better known as the Iron Guard, Romania's fascist movement, an involvement which has brought him much criticism. During the war years, Eliade was outside his homeland, as cultural attaché to its embassies in London and then Lisbon. After the communist takeover of Romania in 1945 he was unable to return. Now apparently non-political, he became a professor of history of religion in the Sorbonne in Paris and, after 1955, at the University of Chicago.[10]

Although controversial, Eliade was undoubtedly the best-known historian of religion of his generation. His prolific output of writings in this area was centered around three basic polarities he saw inform the mentality of *homo religiosus*, as he termed the traditionally religious person: between *illud tempus*, "that time," the Other Time of the Beginning, and our time; between "sacred space" or "sacred time" and ordinary "profane" space and time; and between "cosmic religion" and religions of history. Myth is a major link binding all these dualities together.

The point is that for *homo religiosus* space and time are split-level. People of faith sense a time that once was, but is no more, when God or the gods made the world and all that in it is, when sacred beings were far more visible and accessible than now, when divine and miraculous events happened. All that, though recalled in myth and scripture, has now faded into the light of common day. However, something of the wonder and power of that Other Time can be accessed now through special, set-apart times and spaces: the time of the festival or sacred rite, the space of the temple or church, pilgrimage site, or even that place within reached through prayer, meditation, shamanistic trance, or yoga.

These times and places have a different feel about them; even today, many people sense something special in the air on a great religious holiday like Christmas not felt ordinary days, or in the hushed atmosphere of a great cathedral or temple absent at a regular workaday site. According to Eliade, such sacred places are not simply chosen, but properly were designated by the divine through some sort of hierophany, "sacred showing." So it is that in the precincts of holy places and festivals myths will be told of how they were designated by gods or saints, often in a miraculous way. That decisive divine gesture was made back in *illud tempus*, or at least in the remote past save for sites of recent divine apparitions and miracles (for example Lourdes or Fatima).[11]

As for cosmic and historical religion, the distinction here is between those religions which refer directly back to the *illud tempus* of the creation, and so their sacred times and places are those of nature – the seasons, including seedtime and harvest festivals, sacred mountains and trees, and the like – and those based on later sacred times in history as well, so their sacred times and places will also commemorate historical events and, in a mystical way, endeavor to live in them again. Primal religion generally, and a few other living faiths like Shinto in Japan, as well as much of Hinduism, essentially maintain cosmic religion. But the Axial Age religions are instead historical, so their major festive and sacred space references are to historical moments: the Passover, Last Supper and Cross of Jesus, Mecca as the sacred center in Islam. (Of course these foci, as we have seen, also retain much cosmic religion coloration: Passover, like Easter, is a spring festival; the Christmas tree derives from cosmic-type sacred tree as *axis mundi*, "center of the world" symbolism.)

For Eliade, myth was the connection. In his view, all myth is ultimately creation myth, in the sense that it told where something came from, and thereby validated it. We have seen how he showed that a healing practice, for example, entailed reciting how it was established by a god or primal figure, or how a fisherman identified himself with the primal archetypal fisherman of his culture by using the same gestures, insofar as possible, as he.

JOSEPH CAMPBELL (1904–87)

Joseph Campbell came to his mythological calling by way of literature. A well-rounded student at Columbia, he was an excellent athlete (some thought a potentially Olympic runner) and socially popular as well as a top-ranking student. He followed his undergraduate degree with graduate work in medieval literature, culminating with two years of traveling and studying in Europe during the late 1920s, where he not only worked on the myth of the Holy Grail but, like any bright young man abroad, studied many other things as well. He read James Joyce's *Ulysses* when it was banned in America, and encountered not one but two brief but now legendary epochs in 1920s European culture: the Paris of the famous artists and expatriates like Hemingway, Fitzgerald, Picasso, and Joyce; and the raucous, "decadent," yet feverishly creative Germany of the Weimar republic. In the 1930s Campbell became a professor of literature at Sarah Lawrence College. An early publication, with Henry Morton Robinson, was *A Skeleton Key to Finnegan's Wake* (1944), about that novel by James Joyce.

His own premier mythology book, *The Hero with a Thousand Faces*, came out in 1949. Reviewers liked to point out that its approach, like that of its successors, was essentially that of a literary critic rather than an anthropologist or folklorist. Campbell was quite willing to work with late literary versions of his material, and his real interest was not in scholarly issues, but the meaning of the myth for readers or hearers today.

Like Freud and Jung, Joseph Campbell was convinced that myth was basically about the universal human psyche. The titles of two of his major works, *The Hero with a Thousand Faces* and the three-volume *The Masks of God* say as much.[12] Campbell's accessible books, lectures, and television appearances, together with the work of Jung, did much to popularize the twentieth-century "myth of myth," the notion that the application of mythic models, especially of the hero's journey, to inner life today can be profoundly healing. While Campbell can be, and was, severely criticized by scholars for the cavalier use of his mythological material for his own purposes, perhaps that objective cannot be faulted so long as it is clear this is therapy, not scholarship. Some myths can serve as powerful stimuli to rethink one's own life, undoubtedly, although that is a co-creative venture between the myth and the self. To help in this process was what Campbell set out to do.

RECENT SCHOLARS OF MYTH

Finally, let us refer to a few other names in mythology. Wendy Doniger, Mircea Eliade Distinguished Service Professor in the History of Religions at the University of Chicago, has been particularly interested in how myths provide ways for persons of different cultures to "talk" to one another. In this respect, in books like *Other People's Myths* (1988) and *The Implied Spider* (1998), she has taken a middle path between grand theories like those of Frazer, Freud, Jung, or Campbell, positing a universally common psychic nature to which a "monomyth" responds, and the inevitable reaction that says myths tell nothing except about their own culture.[13] Indeed, it has been charged, as Doniger points out, that such universalist theories, usually based in Euro-American academia, are no more than an intellectual form of colonialism or imperialism, wanting to fit the rest of the world into a mold based in its own form of consciousness.

But, while the post-colonial backlash against the appropriation of the stories of a culture by Euro-Americans who claim to understand what they "really" mean better the native people themselves is understandable, this stance too can be one-sided. Even within a given culture people may vary considerably in their understanding; carried to one extreme, would the anti-imperialist stance suggest that only the teller of a myth can understand it? This would make any communication by means of myth impossible. Or, if it is culture-limited, would it mean that only an Englishman can understand Shakespeare, or a Russian Tolstoy? Surely myth, like all great literature, is broadly human enough to speak of human experience outside its own circle. But the quest for that understanding requires humility, the willingness to start at ground level, and ability to accept limited, imperfect, yet still meaningful results.

Doniger says that comparative mythology in the tradition of Mircea Eliade is viable, but what it requires is not starting off at the top with an all-embracing theory, but at the bottom with myths themselves, listening to them and seeing what they actually tell us about what is common and what is different in the tellers' experience and our own. They are bound to show us that some experiences are indeed generally human, and some culture-bound.

The title of one of her books, *The Implied Spider: Politics and Theology in Myth*, is interesting. The "implied spider" is our shared humanity, that is, the stuff of the Jungian universal archetypes and the Campbellian "monomyth." But, Doniger says, in studying real myths "on the ground" we never actually see the spider; we only get caught up in the webs of such common experiences as birth, sex, death, food, drink. But we suspect, or perhaps only imagine, that if there are webs a spider must be there somewhere.

In addition, it must be noted that, unlike sanguine savants like Campbell who see in myth medicine for the modern world, Doniger is something of a mythological pessimist. To be sure, myths deal with the fundamental problems of human life, but they do not really solve them – that is why we get one myth after another, one religion after another. But we do get many and diverse angles on the vast range of human experience.

Robert A. Segal, in books like *Theories of Myth* (1996), *Theorizing about Myth* (1999) and *Myth: A Very Short Introduction* (2004), is particularly good at summarizing theories of myth from a variety of disciplines, not only history of religion and folkloric, but also social scientific, literary, philosophical, and psychological.[14] He tells us there are three major questions that can be asked of myth: what is it about, what is its origin, and what is its function?[15] Like Doniger, he is modest about the claims of any one theory. Though he prefers a social scientific approach himself, he recognizes that when it comes to analyzing myth, one size does not fit all. Segal is willing to grant that if one theory doesn't work well in a particular case, that it's all right to go to another; in the 2004 work, he studies the myth of Adonis from the perspective of a variety of theories.

Bruce Lincoln, especially in *Theorizing Myth: Narrative, Ideology, and Scholarship* (1999),[16] is interested in the ideological uses of myth, and not only myth itself, but also of mythological scholarship. As we have already noted, he spoke of myth as ideology in narrative form. As an Indo-Europeanist, like William Jones and Georges Dumézil, he is concerned that the mythological heritage of the majority of the peoples of India and Europe has been used in nationalistic, imperialist, racist, and anti-Semitic ways to maintain a sense of difference, and superiority, between these peoples and others, a theme that was very useful in the days of European colonialism, and ever more useful as a basis of the Aryan master-race ideology of German National Socialism.

These explosive ideas cannot be fully dealt with here. It is perhaps sufficient to note (as I did in a review of Lincoln's *Theorizing Myth*), that the scholar in the library, like the scientist in the laboratory, must always bear in mind that what transpires there, arcane and rarefied as it may seem at the time, can have immense consequences.[17] The modern study of comparative mythology, as we have already seen, has had no small impact off campus: together with other causes, it has fueled political movements, justified both oppression and liberation, ignited wars. Whether one agrees with him in every particular, Lincoln makes a good case for taking the consequences of mythology seriously.

William Doty, in *Mythography* (2000, p. 20), is concerned like Segal to provide a list of questions to address mythic texts, recognizing – as seems to be the fashion of recent students – the need to start with myths rather than with theories.[18] He tells us to consider five points: the social, psychological, literary, structural, and political significance of a myth. His writing, moreover, is lively in a way that continually brings home the significance of mythology for understanding what is going on in the world around us today. That brings us to now.

CHAPTER 12

ABSENCE AND LIGHT-SABERS: MODERN MYTH

THE ELUSIVENESS OF MYTH

Myth, like Shambhala and the Grail Castle, is sometimes visible and sometimes not. Writers like Sophia Heller speak of the modern absence of myth, and do not regret its demise. They recognize that the kind of society once held together by public myth, and the sacred kings and official religion that went with it, despite occasional nostalgia is not one in which most people today would really want to live. Heller acknowledges psychologists and scholars like C. G. Jung, Joseph Campbell, James Hillman, and many others who talk of the modern privatization of myth, so that it becomes a vehicle for inward analysis, identity, and therapy. But she does not see exactly why this process needs to employ stories from a very different world to enable healthy modern living; why not instead just use language and examples from contemporary psychology and contemporary life?[1]

If, Heller inquires, myth is given such a different meaning from what it anciently had, is it still myth? Back then, people would say things like, We do things this way because this is the way the ancestors did it, or (as Jung said he was told by Pueblo Indians) if we fail to practice our religion, in ten years the Sun, our Father, would no longer rise.[2] To use the same myth now merely to help one come to terms with one's own inner father, it is said, is hardly the same, and to call modern fantasies like *The Lord of the Rings* or *Star Wars* "mythic" is even more of a stretch; anyone who seriously ate mushrooms because Frodo liked them, or really thought Darth Vader was shadowing him, would be considered highly delusional. Indeed, Heller fears, sometimes too much myth is more the problem than the cure.[3]

On the other hand, James Hillman in effect contends that the modern absence of myth is part of an even greater absence: of a sense of connectedness with the universe, and with the various fragments of our own consciousness. The cause of this loss is the modern depersonalizing of nature – and of any aspect of the self, even our own bodies and imaginations, not under the control of a single "imperial ego." Demythologizing is part and parcel of the loss process, and its sterile final end is loss of the capacity of love anything except our own egos, or egos (whether called God or not) like our own. Hillman quotes Miguel de Unamuno: "In order to love everything, in order to pity everything, human and extra-human, living and non-living, you must feel everything within yourself, you must personalize everything . . . Love personalizes all that it loves."[4]

For Hillman, the soul-vacuum could only be filled by a renewal of "animism," recognizing soul in all that is, then "remythologizing" to let myths tell their stories. Once allowed to speak, they will; for according to Hillman, myth is the natural language of the soul, and of all souls. Soul instinctively casts its ideas, drives, and roles as archetypes – that is, as gods and goddesses – and sees the same equally in the world around. The real question is not "where did the gods come from?" but, "where did the gods that were always there go?" (A modern Pagan, a devotee of ancient Egyptian religion, once said to me, "The gods never died; they just think we did.")

Clearly, between Heller and Hillman – and they can be taken to represent two typical positions on myth – two divergent attitudes obtain, even two concepts of what is meant by truth, not to mention two possible definitions of "myth." (I once added still more confusion, by suggesting that the real myths of a society are those not recognized as myths, and that while myth may still be real the term has become so contaminated we need another word for it.[5])

ABSENCE AND PRESENCE

More issues may be raised. First, as we noted in connection with the savior-hero, it is puzzling that those who speak of the absence or death of myth seem unprepared to recognize it remains alive and almost well in the great religions today, in the founding myths of Judaism, Christianity, Islam, Buddhism, and the myths of the Hindu deities, faiths now listing millions if not billions of believers.

Second, we might again recall that not all stories usually called myths, at least if they are from preliterate peoples and are related to gods, creation, or fundamental social institutions, are necessarily dead serious – "You have to do it exactly the way the ancestors did or there'll be bad trouble." Nor are they even always told the same way. Some, like Coyote, have a certain wry humor yet make pertinent points, cynical as well as solemn, about human life and even the gods – who themselves are often no better than they should be. There is a sense in which ancient myth lives on in Woody Allen as well as *Star Wars* – though the latter also has its comic relief. Again, the question is how wide a net one casts in determining what myth is, then and now.

Third, we could ask if it is not important to take seriously Hillman's contention that depersonalization (of the world and of fragments of the self) is not just a project of the imperial ego, and so biased in its favor. It happens so that the I – the boss I, the No. 1 self – can clear the ground for its own dominance, its own view of the world. So, according to that I, the other "selves" – the one that comes out in dreams, or thinks of being a dancer, sports hero, or great lover, or thinks there really is something lovable in a flower or even a rock – are just fantasies, neuroses, projections, anthropomorphizing. That view may suit No. 1's need for control, but not the contention of Hillman and his archetypal psychology that we and nature do contain within ourselves many voices, many gods, including the call to love and the need to experience fully the many parts we play in the dramas of life.

Myth helps here, Hillman says, because it offers models for these roles. To begin with, consider how we may hold within ourselves something of all the principal characters in a "modern myth" like *Star Wars* – cynical Han Solo, faithful Luke Skywalker, tough yet feminine Princess Leia, even the Shadow, Darth Vader – or all the four companions in *The Wizard of Oz*: the brainy Scarecrow, the loving Tin Woodman, the Cowardly Lion, and of course Dorothy as the consciousness holding them all together. (Of course, these parts are not to be all given completely free rein; that leads to very serious trouble too. Rather, they are to be expressed in ways that are loving, and lead to a full and rich integration of the whole into a harmonious pattern.)

Finally, one could urge that the debate over myth is healthy insofar as it forces us to clarify just how we view reality and the ways we allow our minds to represent it. Do we really want to think about all around us, and ourselves except for a controlling ego, as impersonal, even inert, as so much science and technology, including scientific psychology, in effect does? Or do we want to personify it and make it into a story, then running the risk of the story consuming us till we are only actors in some vast drama, as Plato worried that the tellers of dreams, or myths, might get lost in the dreams and myths and never find their way out? Or is there some place in between?

Eric Weiner, in his exploration of some of the countries whose inhabitants rated highest on a happiness scale, found his way to Iceland, and held conversation there with Larus, a highly accomplished and intellectually sophisticated Icelander, about the reportedly high percentage of his fellow-citizens who believe in elves and dwarfs, the seldom seen "little people" who dwell in that Arctic land's rocky countryside. Larus's answer, given with a twinkle and a "wry smile," was "I don't know if I believe in them, but other people do, and my life is richer for it." After several weeks of thinking about this answer, and trying to figure out just what the hidden life of these descendants of the Vikings was really about, Weiner concluded, "Icelanders, not an especially religious people, occupy the space that exists between not believing and *not* not believing. It is valuable real estate. A place where the door to the unexplained is always left slightly ajar. Just in case."[6]

Finally, we might reflect once more on the twentieth and twenty-first century vogue for novels and films that are, or are said to be, mythic in theme and structure. While Sophia Heller is certainly right in insisting they do not work in exactly the same way as myths told by ancient bards before letters, yet the notion can be repeated that films, at least, are also unlettered, and despite the technology on some deep level of just hearing and seeing a story acted out are not all that different either. Even more to the point, ask this: How does hearing and seeing the mythic story, then and now, affect one's life?

Joseph Campbell, who (regardless of what one think about his scholarship) as much as anyone created the genre of *modern* myth, commented in his famous interviews with Bill Moyers about the appeal of myths. When Moyers asked if myths "are stories of our search through the ages for truth, for meaning, for significance," Campbell answered:

People say that what we're all seeking is a meaning for life. I don't think that's what we're really seeking. I think that what we're seeking is an experience of being alive, so that our life experiences on the purely physical plane will have resonances within our own innermost being and reality, so that we actually feel the rapture of being alive. That's what it's all finally about, and that's what these clues help us to find within ourselves.[7]

Perhaps this is as close as we can come to the mystery of myth past and present. Some have felt that resonance in certain ancient tales of creation, gods, heroes, and the end; some have felt it in modern stories said to be in congruity with them. In the end, we humans are not so disembodied that we can treat of that which moves our innermost being in a purely analytic way. That which makes our "purely physical plane" life feel somehow more alive is worth knowing about. It is hoped that this study of mythology will help in that endeavor.

In Tolkein's *The Lord of the Rings*, when the heroes Frodo and Sam were in desperate straits passing through the Cirith Ungol, Sam wanted to talk about *their* myths, the stories of heroes long past. Then, realizing how their peril and hope was linked to adventures of old, Sam said, "Why, to think of it, we're in the same tale still! It's going on. Don't the great tales never end?"

"No, they never end as tales," said Frodo, "but the people in them come, and go when their part's ended. Our part will end later – or sooner."[8]

NOTES

CHAPTER 1

1 Philippi, Donald L. (trans.), *Kojiki*. Tokyo: University of Tokyo Press, 1968, pp. 49–70.
2 See Csapo, Eric, *Theories of Mythology*. Oxford and Malden, MA: Blackwell, 2005.
3 Philippi, *Kojiki*; Aston, A.W.G. (trans.), *Nihongi*. London: Allen & Unwin, 1968.
4 Lévi-Strauss, Claude, *The Raw and the Cooked*. John and Doreen Weightman (trans.). New York: Harper, 1969.
5 "Book of Invasions, The Book of Leinster Redaction." *Irish Texts Archive*, www.ancienttexts.org/library/celtic/irish. For a summary see Fleming, Fergus, Shahrukh Husain, C. Scott Littleton, Linda A. Malcor; and Duncan Baird (Corporate Author), *Heroes of the Dawn: Celtic Myth*. Amsterdam: Time-Life Books, 1996, pp. 38–9.
6 Philippi, *Kojiki*, pp. 74–92; Aston, *Nihongi*, pp. 33–59.
7 Berger, Peter, *The Sacred Canopy*. Garden City, NY: Doubleday, 1969, p. 28.
8 Segal, Robert A., *Joseph Campbell: An Introduction*. New York; Garland, 1987, p. 137.

CHAPTER 2

1 Tolkien, J. R. R., *The Annotated Hobbit*. Annotated by Douglas A. Anderson. Boston: Houghton Mifflin, 1966, p. 219.
2 Spencer, Baldwin, and F. J. Gillen, *The Native Tribes of Central Australia*. London: Macmillan, 1938, pp. 388–91. For a critical discussion of this account, see Sam Gill, *Storytracking*. New York: Oxford University Press, 1998, pp. 9–17.
3 Christie, Anthony, *Chinese Mythology*. London: Hamlyn, 1968, pp. 49–53. Anne Birrell, *Chinese Mythology: An Introduction*. Baltimore: Johns Hopkins University Press, 1993, pp. 31–3, suggests the egg image, which appears only in later sources, is literary metaphor rather than mythology.

4 Leeming, David Adams, *The World of Myth: An Anthology*. New York: Oxford University Press, 1990, pp. 147–53.

5 Davidson, H. R. Ellis, *Gods and Myths of Northern Europe*. Baltimore: Penguin Books, 1964, pp. 28–31, 51.

6 Clark, Peter, *Zoroastrianism*. Brighton, UK: Sussex Academic Press, 1998, pp. 59–65; Mary Boyce, *Zoroastrians: Their Beliefs and Practices*. London: Routledge and Kegan Paul, 1979, pp. 27–9.

7 Boyce, *Ibid.*

8 Inagaki, Hisao (trans.), *The Three Pure Land Sutras*. Berkeley, CA: Numata Center for Buddhist Translations and Research, 2003.

9 Steward, Desmond, *Mecca*. New York: Newsweek Book Division, 1980.

10 Eliade, Mircea, *The Sacred and the Profane*. Willard R. Trask (trans.). New York: Harcourt Brace Jovanovich, 1959.

11 Courlander, Harold, *Tales of Yoruba Gods and Heroes*. New York: Crown, 1973, pp. 18–21.

12 Frazer, James G., *The Belief in Immortality*. London: Macmillan, 1913, I, pp. 72–3.

CHAPTER 3

1 On Euhermerism see Leonard, Scott, and Michael McClure, *Myth and Knowing*. Boston: McGraw-Hill, 2004, pp. 4–5, and William Doty, *Mythography*. Tuscaloosa: University of Alabama Press, 2nd edn 2000, p. 10.

2 Lyotard, Jean-François, *The Postmodern Condition: A Report on Knowledge*. Geoff Bennington and Brian Massumi (trans.). Minneapolis: University of Minnesota Press, 1984, p. ix.

3 Frazer, Sir James, *The Golden Bough*. 3rd edn, 12 vols, London: Macmillan, 1906–15; *The Golden Bough: A New Abridgment from the Second and Third Editions*. Oxford: Oxford World's Classics Series, 2003, are among the several editions of this work, first published in two volumes in 1890; Robert Ackerman, *J.G. Frazer, His Life and Work*. Cambridge: Cambridge University Press, 1987. See also Ackerman, *The Myth and Ritual School: J. G. Frazer and the Cambridge Ritualists*. 2nd edn, New York and London: Routledge, 2002.

4 René Girard, *Violence and the Sacred*. Patrick Gregory (trans.). Baltimore: Johns Hopkins University Press, 1972; *Things Hidden Since the Foundation of the World*. Stephan Bann and Michael Metteer (trans.). Palo Alto, CA: Stanford University Press, 1987.

5 Malinowski, Bronislaw, *Myth in Primitive Psychology*. London: Routledge, 1926, and other works.

6 Lévi-Strauss, Claude, *The Raw and the Cooked*. John and Doreen Weightman (trans.). Chicago: University of Chicago Press, 1990, and other works.

7 Sigmund Freud's three books on religion are *Totem and Taboo*. New York: New Republic, 1927; *The Future of an Illusion*. New York: Liveright, 1928, and *Moses and Monotheism*. New York:

Knopf, 1939. The bibliography of works discussing Freud and religion is extensive.

8 The best introduction to Géza Róheim's voluminous work is probably Paul A. Robinson, *The Freudian Left: Wilhelm Reich, Géza Róheim, Herbert Marcuse*. New York: Harper & Row, 1969, pp. 75–146.

9 An accessible introduction to Jung and myth is Carl G. Jung, *Man and his Symbols*. Garden City, NY: Doubleday, 1964.

10 Hillman, James, *Re-Visioning Psychology*. New York: Harper Perennial, 1992, p. 99. 1st edn 1976.

11 Martin, Charles, *Metamorphoses: A New Translation*. New York: W. W. Norton, 2005; for commentary see Elaine Fantham, *Ovid's Metamorphoses*. New York: Oxford University Press, 2004.

12 See Fugate, Joe K., *The Psychological Basis of Herder's Aesthetics*. The Hague: Mouton, 1966, pp. 110–19

13 Beach, Edward Allen, *The Potencies of God(s): Schelling's Philosophy of Mythology*. Albany: SUNY Press, 1994.

14 Grottanelli, Cristiano, "Nietzsche and Myth," *History of Religions*, 37, 1 (Aug. 1997), pp. 3–20.

15 Campbell, Joseph, *Myths to Live By*. New York: Viking, 1972, p. 214.

16 See Brisson, Luc, *Plato the Myth Maker*, Gerard Naddaf (trans.). Chicago: University of Chicago Press, 1998.

17 Heller, Sophia, *The Absence of Myth*. Albany: SUNY, 2006.

18 Back cover statement by William Doty for Sophia Heller, *The Absence of Myth, op. cit.*, hardcover edition.

19 Ellwood, Robert, *The Politics of Myth: A Study of C.G. Jung, Mircea Eliade, and Joseph Campbell*. Albany: SUNY Press, 1999; Ellwood, "Is Mythology Obsolete?" *Journal of the American Academy of Religion*, Vol. 69, No. 3 (September 2002), pp. 673–86.

20 Lincoln, Bruce, *Theorizing Myth*. University of Chicago Press, 1999, p. 207.

21 Ellwood, "Is Mythology Obsolete?", p. 675.

CHAPTER 4

1 Lowenstein, Tom, *Ancient Land, Sacred Whale*. New York: Farrar, Straus and Giroux, 1994, p. 3.

2 Hesiod, *Theogony and Works and Days*. Stanley Lombardo and Robert Lamberton (trans.). Indianapolis: Hackett, 1993, pp. 64–6.

3 Ovid, *Metamorphoses*. Charles Martin (trans.). New York: Norton, 2004, p. 15.

4 Hesiod, *Theogony and Works and Days*, pp. 25–6.

5 Heidel, Alexander, *The Babylonian Genesis: The Story of Creation*. Chicago: University of Chicago, 1963.

6 Weiss, Gerald, *Campa Cosmology: The World of a Forest Tribe*. New York: American Museum of Natural History, 1975.

7 Dimmitt, Cornelia, and J. A. B. van Buitenen (trans.), *Classical Hindu Mythology: A Reader in the Sanskrit Puranas*, Philadelphia: Temple

University Press, 1978, pp. 30–1; Kinsley, David R., *Hinduism: A Cultural Perspective*, 2nd edn. Englewood Cliffs, NJ: Prentice Hall, 1963, p. 63; A. L. Dallapiccola, *Hindu Myths*. London: British Museum Press, 2003, p. 19.

8 Norbu, Tubten Jigme, and Colin M. Turnbull, *Tibet*. New York: Simon and Schuster, 1968, p. 19.

9 Khan, Noor Inayat, *Twenty Jātaka Tales*. Rochester VT: Inner Traditions, 1975.

10 Campion, Nicholas, *The Great Year: Astrology, Millenarianism, and History in the Western Tradition*. London and New York: Arkana, 1994.

11 Alpers, Antony, *Legends of the South Seas*. New York: Crowell, 1970, pp. 51–4.

12 Chatwin, Bruce, *The Songlines*. New York: Viking, 1987, p. 11.

13 Mohawk, John, *The Iroquois Creation Story*. Buffalo, NY: Mohawk Publications, 2005; John Bierhorst, *The Woman Who Fell from the Sky: The Iroquois Story of Creation*. New York: Morrow, 1993.

14 *The Vishnu Purana*. H. H. Wilson (trans.). Calcutta: Punthi Pustak, 1961 (1st edn 1840), pp. 25–6; Daniélou, Jean, *Hindu Polytheism*. New York: Pantheon, 1964, p. 168.

15 Bailey, Greg, *The Mythology of Brahma*. New York: Oxford University Press, 1983, pp. 119–20.

16 Norbu & Turnbull, *Tibet*, p. 28.

17 Lowenstein, *Ancient Land, Sacred Whale*, pp. 5–9.

18 Cruikshank, Julie, *Life Lived Like a Story: Life Stories of Three Yukon Tribal Elders*. Lincoln: University of Nebraska Press, 1990, pp. 282–8.

19 Riordan, James, *The Sun Maiden and the Crescent Moon: Siberian Folk Tales*. Edinburgh: Canongate, 1989, pp. 42–8.

CHAPTER 5

1 Riches, Samantha, *St. George: Hero, Martyr, and Myth*. Sutton: Thrupp UK, 2000.

2 Heaney, Seamus, *Beowulf: A Verse Translation*. New York; Norton, 2002.

3 *The Bhagavad-Gita: The Song of God*. Swami Prabhavananda and Christopher Isherwood (trans.). Hollywood, CA: Vedanta Press, 1944, 1987, pp. 41–2.

4 Benedict, Ruth, *The Chrysanthemum and the Sword*. Boston: Houghton Mifflin, 1946.

5 Some observations in these paragraphs are suggested by John Lash, *The Hero: Manhood and Power*. London: Thames and Hudson, 1990, pp. 5–15.

6 Kerényi, C., *The Heroes of the Greeks*. H. J. Rose (trans.). London: Thames & Hudson, 1959, pp. 128–208.

7 Birrell, Anne, *Chinese Mythology: An Introduction*. Baltimore: Johns Hopkins University Press, 1993, pp. 138–45; Yang Lihui and Deming

An, with Jessica Anderson Turner, *Handbook of Chinese Mythology.* Santa Barbara, CA: ABC-CLIO, 2005, pp. 230–4.

8 David-Neel, Alexandra, and the Lama Yongden, *The Superhuman Life of Gesar of Ling.* New York: Kendall, 1934.

9 Numerous studies of the Grail mythology are available. See Richard Barber, *The Holy Grail: Imagination and Belief.* Cambridge, MA: Harvard University Press, 2004, for a good introduction and bibliography.

10 Baum, L. Frank, *The Wonderful Wizard of Oz.* Chicago: Hill, 1900.

CHAPTER 6

1 Campbell, Joseph, *The Hero with a Thousand Faces.* New York: Bollengen Foundation, 1949.

2 Jaspers, Karl, *The Origin and Goal of History.* Michael Bullock (trans.). London: Routledge & Kegan Paul, 1953, pp. 1–27, 51–60.

3 Eliade, Mircea, *Cosmos and History.* Willard R. Trask (trans.). New York: Harper & Row, 1959. Originally pub. as *The Myth of the Eternal Return.* New York: Pantheon Books, 1954.

4 *Ibid.*, Ch. 4.

5 See Bryant, Edwin F. (ed.), *Krishna: A Sourcebook.* New York: Oxford University Press, 2007; David R. Kinsley, *The Sword and the Flute.* Berkeley: University of California Press, 1975; Milton Singer (ed.), *Krishna: Myths, Rites, and Attitudes.* Chicago: University of Chicago Press, 1968.

6 See King, Karen, *The Gospel of Mary of Magdala: Jesus and the First Woman Apostle.* Santa Rosa, CA: Polebridge Press, 2003.

7 Percheron, Maurice, *The Marvelous Life of the Buddha.* New York: St. Martin's Press, 1960, is a readable telling of the traditional story. See also Karen Armstrong, *Buddha.* New York: Penguin, 2001.

8 Weber, Max, *The Sociology of Religion.* Boston: Beacon, 1963, p. 55.

9 Armstrong, Karen, *Muhammad: A Biography of the Prophet.* HarperSanFrancisco, 1992. Martin Forward, *Muhammad: A Short Biography.* Oxford: Oneworld, 1997.

10 Heller, Sophia, *The Absence of Myth*, Albany: SUNY Press, 2006, p. 204. See the discussion pp. 204–7.

CHAPTER 7

1 Ferry, David, *Gilgamesh: A New Rendering in English Verse.* New York: Farrar, Strauss and Giraudoux, 1993.

2 Spencer, A. J., *Death in Ancient Egypt.* Harmondsworth: Penguin, 1982.

3 Rees, Alwyn and Brinley Rees, *Celtic Heritage: Ancient Traditions of Ireland and Wales.* New York: Grove Press, 1961.

4 Bauer, Wolfgang, *China and the Search for Happiness.* New York: Seabury, 1976.

5 Davidson, H. R. Ellis, *Gods and Myths of Northern Europe*. Baltimore, MD: Penguin, 1964.

6 Deacon, A. Bernard, *Malekula: A Vanishing People in the New Hebrides*. London: Routledge, 1924.

7 Alexander, H. B., *North American Mythology*. Boston: Marshall Jones, 1916, pp. 147–9.

8 Eliade, Mircea, *Shamanism: Archaic Techniques of Ecstasy*. Willard R. Trask (trans.). New York: Pantheon Books, 1964, pp. 60–1. Based on Knud Rasmussen, *Intellectual Culture of the Iglulik Eskimos*. William Worster (trans.). Copenhagen, 1930, pp. 111 ff.

9 Birnbaum, Edwin, *The Way to Shamabhala*. Garden City, NY: Doubleday Anchor Books, 1980.

10 Figes, Orlando, *Natasha's Dance: A Cultural History of Russia*. New York: Henry Holt, 2002, pp. 308–9.

11 Basham, A. L., *The Wonder that Was India*. New York: Hawthorne, 1963, p. 309; Veronica Ions, *Hindu Mythology*. London: Paul Hamlyn, 1967, p. 72.

12 Sponberg, Alan and Helen Hardacre (eds), *Maitreya: The Future Buddha*. New York: Cambridge University Press, 1988.

13 See Bernbaum, Edwin, *The Way to Shambhala*. Los Angeles: Tarcher, 1989, pp. 237–45.

14 LaHaye, Tim, and Jerry B. Jenkins, *Left Behind* (1995), *Tribulation Force* (1996), *Nicolae* (1997), *Soul Harvest* (1998), *Apollyon* (1999), *Assassins* (1999b), *The Indwelling* (2000), *The Mark* (2000b), *Desecration* (2001). *The Remnant* (2002), *Armageddon* (2003), *Glorious Appearing* (2004). All Wheaton: IL: Tyndale.

15 Shuck, Glenn W., *Marks of the Beast: The* Left Behind *Novels and the Struggle for Evangelical Identity*. Albany: SUNY Press, 2005.

16 Lifton, Robert Jay, *Revolutionary Immortality*. New York: Random House, 1968.

17 Marcuse, Herbert, *Eros and Civilization*. Boston: Beacon Press, 1968, p. 233. Cited from Walter Benjamin.

18 Green, Harvey, *The Light of the Home: An Intimate View of the Lives of Women in Victorian Ameria*. New York: Pantheon, 1983, pp. 164–79. For the novels see Elizabeth Stuart Phelps, *Three Spiritualist Novels*. Urbana and Chicago: University of Illinois Press, 2000.

CHAPTER 8

1 Handelman, Don, "The Ritual-Clown: Attributes and Affinities," *Anthropos* 76 (1981), pp. 321–70; Wolfgang M. Zucker, "The Clown as the Lord of Disorder," in M. Conrad Hyers (ed.), *Holy Laughter*. New York: Seabury, 1969. This essay emphasizes the clown as disrupter or outsider, and the Feast of Fools type of performance. See also William J. Hynes and William G. Doty (eds), *Mythical Trickster Figures*. Tuscaloosa: University of Alabama Press, 1993, with extensive bibliography.

2 Werner, Alice, *Myths and Legends of the Bantu*. London: Cass, 1968, pp. 30–1.
3 Finnegan, Ruth, *Limba Stories and Story-Telling*. Oxford: Clarendon Press, 1967, p. 234–5.
4 J. R. R. Tolkien, *The Fellowship of the Ring*. 2nd edition, Boston: Houghton Mifflin, 1965, p. 65.
5 Thubron, Colin, *Shadows of the Silk Road*. New York: HarperCollins, 2007, p. 264.
6 Kerrigan, Michael, Charles Phillips, and Duncan Baird (Corporate Author), *Forests of the Vampire: Slavic Myth*. Amsterdam: Time-Life Books, 1999, pp. 117–18.
7 Shipley, William, *The Maidu Indian Myths and Stories of Hánc'ibyjim*. Berkeley, CA: Heyday Books, 1991, pp. 51–2.
8 *The Epic of Gilgamesh*, Benjamin R. Foster (ed. and trans.). New York: Norton, 2001. Also contains Sumerian and Hittite Gilgamesh material.
9 Birrell, Anne, *Chinese Mythology: An Introduction*. Baltimore: Johns Hopkins University Press, 1993, pp. 146–59; Yang Lihui and Deming An, with Jessica Anderson Turner, *Handbook of Chinese Mythology*. Santa Barbara, CA: ABC-CLIO, 2005, pp. 237–40; Mark Edward Lewis, *The Flood Myths of Early China*. Albany: SUNY Press, 2006. For an overall presentation of world flood myths, see Alan Dundes (ed.), *The Flood Myth*. Berkeley: University of California Press, 1988.

CHAPTER 9

1 Gray, John, *Black Mass: Apocalyptic Religion and the Death of Utopia*. New York: Farrar, Straus and Giroux, 2007, p. 1.
2 For a fascinating study see Mark Girouard, *The Return to Camelot: Chivalry and the English Gentleman*. London and New Haven, CT: Yale University Press, 1981.
3 Wyman, Leland C., *Blessingway: With Three Versions of the Myth*. Tucson, AZ: University of Arizona Press, 1970. See also Louise Lamphere and Marilyn Notah Verney, "Navajo Religious Traditions," *Encyclopedia of Religion*, 2nd edn. Farmington Hills, MI: Macmillan Reference, 2005, vol. 9, pp. 6, 441–3.
4 Kleinert, Sylvia and Margo Neale, *The Oxford Companion to Aboriginal Art and Culture*. South Melbourne, Australia; Mircea Eliade, *Australian Religions: An Introduction*. Ithaca, NY: Cornell University Press, 1973, Chapter 2, "Culture Heroes and Mythical Geography."
5 Hay, Robert P., "George Washington: American Moses," *American Quarterly*, 21, 4 (Winter 1969), pp. 780–91.
6 Cherry, Conrad, *God's New Israel: Religious Interpretations of American Destiny*. Chapel Hill: University of North Carolina Press, rev. edn, 1998.
7 Fagles, Robert (trans.), *The Aeneid*. New York: Viking, 2006.
8 Cannon, Garland, *The Life and Mind of Oriental Jones: Sir William Jones, the Father of Modern Linguistics*. Cambridge University Press,

1980; Bruce Lincoln, *Theorizing Myth: Narrative, Ideology, and Scholarship*. Chicago: University of Chicago Press, 1999.

9 See Lincoln, *op. cit.*, and George L. Mosse, *The Crisis of German Ideology: Intellectual Origins of the Third Reich*. New York: Gosset and Dunlap, 1964.

10 See Sternhall, Zeev, *The Birth of Fascist Ideology*. Princeton University Press, 1994, especially Chapter 1, "George Sorel and the Antimaterialist Revision of Marxism," and Mark Antliff, *Avant-garde Fascism: The Mobilization of Myth, Art, and Culture in France 1909–1939*, Durham: Duke University Press, 2007, with valuable references to Sorel throughout.

11 Riefenstahl, Leni, *The Slave of Time*. London: Quartet Books, 1992, p. 101.

12 Quoted in Wilbur M. Fridell, "Government Ethics Textbooks in Late Meiji Japan," *Journal of Asian Studies* (August 1970), p. 831. See also Kenneth B. Pyle, *The Making of Modern Japan*. Lexington, MA: D. C. Heath and Co., 1978.

13 Hall, Robert King and John Owen Gauntlett, *Kokutai no Hongi; Cardinal Principles of the National Entity of Japan*. Cambridge, MA: Harvard University Press, 1949.

14 Cited in Robert Bellah, *Imagining Japan*. Berkeley, CA: University of California Press, 2003, p. 183.

CHAPTER 10

1 Hillman, James, *The Dream and the Underworld*. New York: Harper & Row, 1979, p. 23.

2 Avens, Robert, *Imaginal Body*. Washington, DC: University Press of America, 1982, p. 76; Owen Barfield, *The Rediscovery of Meaning and Other Essays*. Middleton, CT: Wesleyan University Press, 1977, p. 75.

3 Campbell, Joseph, *The Hero with a Thousand Faces*. New York: Bollengen Foundation, 1949, p. vii.

4 Campbell, Joseph, *The Masks of God: Primitive Mythology*. New York: Viking Press, 1959, pp. 68–71, 77.

5 Hillman, *Ibid.*, p. 18.

6 Franz, Marie-Luise von, *An Introduction to the Psychology of Fairy Tales*. Zürich: Spring Publications, 1975, pp. 145–7.

7 Hillman, James, *Re-Visioning Psychology*. New York: HarperCollins, 1975.

8 Hillman, *Dream and the Underworld*, pp. 25, 27–32.

9 Avens, Roberts, *Imagination Is Reality: Western Nirvana in Jung, Hillman, Barfield and Cassirer*. Dallas: Spring Publications, 1980; and *Imaginal Body: Para-Jungian Reflections on Soul, Imagination, and Death*. Washington, DC: University Press of America, 1982.

10 Beach, Edward Allen, *The Potencies of God(s): Schelling's Philosophy of Mythology*. Albany: SUNY Press, 1994.

11 Huxley, Aldous, *The Doors of Perception and Heaven and Hell*. New

York: Harper Perennial Library edition, 1990, pp. 84–5. First published 1956.

12 Wolf, Maryanne, *Proust and the Squid: The Story and Science of the Reading Brain*. New York: Harper, 2007. This book and related considerations are well reviewed in Caleb Crain, "Twilight of the Books," *The New Yorker*, Dec. 24 & 31, 2007, pp. 134–9.

13 Summarized in Ong, Walter J., *Orality and Literacy: The Technologizing of the Word*. New York: Routledge, 1982, pp. 49–56. See Aleksandr Romanovich Luria, *Cognitive Development: Its Cultural and Social Foundations*. Martin Lopez-Morillas and Lynn Solotaroff (trans.). Cambridge, MA: Harvard University Press, 1976.

14 Ong, Walter J., *Orality and Literacy*, pp. 43–5.

15 Havelock, Eric A., *The Literate Revolution in Greece and its Cultural Consequences*. Princeton University Press, 1982, pp. 179. See also Havelock, *Preface to Plato*. Cambridge, MA: Harvard University Press, 1963, especially Part I, "The Image-Thinkers," on oral versus written epic and knowledge.

CHAPTER 11

1 Herder, Johann Gottfried von, *Outlines of a Philosophy of the History of Man*. T. Churchill (trans.). New York: Bergman, n.d., fasc. of ed. of London, 1800. See especially pp. 194–201.

2 Schelling, Friedrich W. J., *The Ages of the World*. Frederick de Wolfe Bolman, Jr. (trans.). New York: Columbia University Press, 1942, especially pp. 77, 93n. See also Paul Tillich, *The Construction of the History of Religion in Schelling's Positive Philosophy*. Translation and Introduction by Victor Nuovo. Lewisburg, PA: Bucknell University Press, 1974.

3 See Cristiano Grottanelli, "Nietzsche and Myth," *History of Religions*, Vol. 37, No. 1 (August 1997), pp. 3–20.

4 Frazer, Sir James, *The Golden Bough*, 3rd edn, 12 vols, London: Macmillan, 1906–15; *The Golden Bough: A New Abridgment from the Second and Third Editions*. Oxford: Oxford World's Classics Series, 2003, are among the several editions of this work, first published in two volumes in 1890.

5 See also Robert Ackerman, *J.G. Frazer, His Life and Work*. Cambridge University Press, 1987; Ackerman, *The Myth and Ritual School: J. G. Frazer and the Cambridge Ritualists*. 2nd edn, New York and London: Routledge, 2002; and John B. Vickery, *The Literary Impact of "The Golden Bough."* Princeton University Press, 1973.

6 Cassirer, Ernst, *The Philosophy of Symbolic Forms*, 4 vols. Ralph Manheim (trans.). New Haven: Yale University Press, 1953; *Essays on Language, Myth, and Art*. New Haven: Yale University Press, 2008, pp. 73, 76, 77.

7 Cassirer, Ernst, *An Essay on Man*. New Haven: Yale University Press, 1944, pp. 73–7.

8 Langer, Susanne, *Philosophy in a New Key*. Cambridge, MA: Harvard University Press, 1942, p. 171.

9 For Georges Dumézil, see C. Scott Littleton, *The New Comparative Mythology*. Berkeley: University of California Press, 1982.
10 See Robert Ellwood, *The Politics of Myth: A Study of C.G. Jung, Mircea Eliade, and Joseph Campbell*. Albany. NY: SUNY Press, 1999, Chapter 3, "Mircea Eliade and Nostalgia for the Sacred,"; and Bryan Rennie, *Reconstructing Eliade*, Albany, NY: SUNY Press, 1996, Chapter 13, "Eliade's Political Involvement."
11 Eliade, Mircea, *The Sacred and the Profane*, Transl. Willard R. Trask. New York: Harcourt Brace Jovanovich, 1959; *The Myth of the Eternal Return*. Willard R. Trask (trans.). New York: Pantheon, 1954 (also published as *Cosmos and History*); *Myth and Reality*, Willard R. Trask (trans.). New York: Harper & Row, 1963.
12 Campbell, Joseph, *The Hero with a Thousand Faces*. New York: Pantheon, 1949. *The Masks of God*. Vol. 1, *Primitive Mythology*. New York: Viking, 1959; vol. 2, *Oriental Mythology*. New York: Viking, 1962; vol. 3, *Occidental Mythology*. New York: Viking, 1964; vol. 4, *Creative Mythology*. New York: Viking, 1968.
13 Doniger, Wendy, *Other People's Myths: The Cave of Echoes*. New York: Macmillan, 1988 (as Wendy Doniger O'Flaherty); *The Implied Spider: Politics and Theology in Myth*. New York: Columbia University Press, 1998.
14 Segal, Robert S., *Theorizing About Myth*. Amherst, MA: University of Massachusetts Press, 1999; *Myth: A Very Short Introduction*. New York: Oxford University Press, 2004.
15 Segal, *Theorizing About Myth*, p. 67.
16 Lincoln, Bruce, *Theorizing Myth*. University of Chicago Press, 2000.
17 Ellwood, Robert, "Is Mythology Obsolete?" *Journal of the American Academy of Religion*, Vol. 69, No. 3 (September 2002), pp. 673–86.
18 Doty, William, *Mythography*. Tuscaloosa: University of Alabama Press, 2nd edn, 2000.

CHAPTER 12

1 Heller, Sophia, *The Absence of Myth*. Albany: SUNY Press, 2006, pp. 217–21.
2 Jung, C. G., *Memories, Dreams, Reflections*. Trans. Richard and Clara Winston. New York: Random House, 1961, p. 252. Cited Heller, *Absence of Myth*, pp. 13–14.
3 Heller, *Absence of Myth*, p. 2.
4 Unamuno, Miguel de, *The Tragic Sense of Life*. Transl. J. E. C. Fitch. New York: Dover, 1954, p. 139, Cited James Hillman, *Rev-Visioning Psychology*. New York: Harper & Row, 1976, p. 15.
5 Ellwood, Robert, *The Politics of Myth: A Study of C.G. Jung, Mircea Eliade, and Joseph Campbell*. Albany: SUNY Press, 1999; Ellwood, "Is Mythology Obsolete?" *Journal of the American Academy of Religion*, Vol. 69, No. 3 (September 2002), pp. 673–86.

NOTES

6 Weiner, Eric, *The Geography of Bliss*. New York and Boston: Twelve, 2008, p. 168.
7 Campbell, Joseph, with Bill Moyers, *The Power of Myth*. New York: Doubleday, 1985, p. 5.
8 Tokien, J. R. R., *The Two Towers*. Boston: Houghton, Mifflin, 1954, p. 321.

FURTHER READING

GENERAL COLLECTIONS OF MYTHS AND REFERENCE WORKS

Aldington, R., and D. Ames (trans.), *New Larousse Encyclopdia of Mythology*. Lanond; Hamlyn, 1968.

Baird, Duncan, Publisher, *Myth and Mankind*. 20 vols. Amsterdam: Time-Life Books, 1996–2000.

Bently, Peter (ed.), *The Dictionary of World Myth*. New York: Facts on File, 1995.

Bulfinch, Thomas, *Bulfinch's Mythology*. 2 vols. New York: Mentor, 1962.

Doty, William G., *Myth: A Handbook*. Wesport, CT: Greenwood, 2004.

Dundes, Alan, ed., *The Flood Myth*. Berkeley: University of California Press, 1988.

Frazer, Sir James, *The Golden Bough*. 3rd edn, 12 vols, London: Macmillan, 1906–15.

Gray, Louis H., and George Foot Moore, eds., *Mythology of All Races*. 13 vols. Boston: Marshall Jones, 1916–32.

Leeming, David Adams, *The World of Myth: An Anthology*. New York: Oxford University Press, 1990.

Mercante, Anthony S., *The Facts on File Encyclopedia of World Mythology and Legend*. 2nd edition rev. by James R. Dow. 2 vols., New York: Facts on File, 2004.

Phillips, Ellen (ed.), *The Enchanted World*. 20 vols. Alexandria, VA: Time-Life Books, 1984.

Rosenberg, Donna, *Folklore, Myths, and Legends*. Boston: McGraw-Hill, 1997.

——, *World Mythology: An Anthology of the Great Myths and Epics*. 3rd ed., Boston: McGraw-Hill, 2001.

EXEMPLARY COLLECTIONS AND STUDIES OF MYTH IN PARTICULAR CULTURES

Afanas'ev, Aleksander, *Russian Folk Tales*. New York: Random House, 1980.

Bonnefoy, Yves, with Wendy Doniger (trans.), *Asian Mythologies*. University of Chicago Press, 1993.

Buxton, Richard, *The Complete World of Greek Mythology*. New York: Thames & Hudson, 2004.

Christie, Anthony, *Chinese Mythology*. London: Hamlyn, 1968.

Davidson, H. R. Ellis, *Gods and Myths of Northern Europe*. Baltimore: Penguin Books, 1964.

Finnegan, Ruth, *Limba Stories and Story-Telling*. Oxford: Clarendon Press, 1967, p. 234–35.

Osborne, Harold, *South American Mythology*. Newnes: Feltham, 1990.

Rees, Alwyn and Brinley Rees, *Celtic Heritage: Ancient Traditions of Ireland and Wales*. New York: Grove Press, 1961.

Riordan, James, *The Sun Maiden and the Crescent Moon: Siberian Folk Tales*. Edinburgh: Canongate, 1989.

Simpson, Jacqueline, *European Mythology*. London: Hamlyn, 1987.

CREATION MYTHS

Bierhorst, John, *The Woman Who Fell from the Sky: The Iroquois Story of Creation*. New York: Morrow, 1993.

Brandon, S. G. F., *Creation Legends of the Ancient Near East*. London: Hodder and Stoughton, 1963.

Eliade, Mircea, *Gods, Goddesses and Myths of Creation*. New York: Harper & Row, 1974.

Farmer, P. (ed.), *Beginnings: Creation Myths of the World*. New York: Atheneum, 1979.

Guthrie, W. K. C., *In the Beginning: Some Greek Views on the Origins of Life and the Early State of Man*. Ithaca, NY: Cornell University Press, 1957.

Heidel, Alexander, *The Babylonian Genesis: The Story of Creation*. Chicago: University of Chicago Press, 1963.

Leeming, David, with Margaret Leeming. *A Dictionary of Creation Myths*. New York: Oxford University Press, 1994.

Long, Charles H., *Alpha: The Myths of Creation*. New York; Braziller, 1963.

Sproul, Barbara C., *Primal Myth: Creating the World*. San Francisco: Harper & Row, 1979

Weigle, Marta. *Creation and Procreation; Feminist Reflections on Mythologies of Cosmogony and Parturition*. Philadelphia: University of Pennsylvania Press, 1989.

HERO MYTHS

Armstrong, Karen, *Muhammad: A Biography of the Prophet*. HarperSanFrancisco, 1992.

Barber, Richard, *The Holy Grail: Imagination and Belief*. Cambridge, MA: Harvard University Press, 2004.

Campbell, Joseph, *The Hero with a Thousand Faces*. New York: Bollingen Foundation, 1949.

David-Neel, Alexandra, and the Lama Yongden, *The Superhuman Life of Gesar of Ling*. New York: Kendall, 1934.

Fagles, Robert (trans.), *The Aeneid*. New York: Viking, 2006.

Heaney, Seamus, *Beowulf: A Verse Translation*. New York; Norton, 2002.

Kerényi, C., *The Heroes of the Greeks*. H. J. Rose (trans.). London: Thames & Hudson, 1959.

Percheron, Maurice, *The Marvelous Life of the Buddha*. New York: St. Martin's Press, 1960.

Raglan, Lord Fitzroy, *The Hero*. London: Watts, 1949.

Riches, Samantha, *St. George: Hero, Martyr, and Myth*. Thrupp UK: Sutton, 2000.

WORKS ON MYTHOLOGICAL THEORY

Cassirer, Ernst, *Essays on Language, Myth, and Art*. New Haven: Yale University Press, 2008, pp. 73, 76, 77.

Csapo, Eric, *Theories of Mythology*. Oxford and Malden, MA: Blackwell, 2005.

Doniger, Wendy, *The Implied Spider: Politics and Theology in Myth*. New York: Columbia University Press, 1998.

Doty, William, *Mythography*. Tuscaloosa: University of Alabama Press, 2nd edn. 2000.

Eliade, Mircea, *Myth and Reality*. New York: Harper and Row, 1963.

Heller, Sophia, *The Absence of Myth*. Albany: SUNY Press, 2006.

Leonard, Scott, and Michael McClure, *Myth and Knowing*. Boston: McGraw-Hill, 2004.

Lévi-Strauss, Claude, *The Raw and the Cooked*. Trans. John and Doreen Weightman. New York: Harper, 1969.

Lincoln, Bruce, *Theorizing Myth*. Chicago: University of Chicago Press, 1999.

Segal, Robert S., *Theorizing About Myth*. Amherst, MA: University of Massachusetts Press.

THE PSYCHOLOGY OF MYTH

Avens, Roberts, *Imagination Is Reality: Western Nirvana in Jung, Hillman, Barfield and Cassirer*. Dallas: Spring Publications, 1980.

Bolles, Kees W., *The Freedom of Man in Myth*. Nashville: Vanderbilt University Press, 1993.

Eliade, Mircea, *Cosmos and History*. Willard R. Trask (trans.). New York: Harper & Row, 1959. Originally pub. as *The Myth of the Eternal Return*. New York: Pantheon Books, 1954.

Freud, Sigmund, *Totem and Taboo*. New York: New Republic, 1918, 1927.

Hillman, James, *Rev-Visioning Psychology*. New York: Harper and Row, 1976.

Jung, C. G., *Jung on Mythology*. Robert A. Segal (ed.). Princeton University Press, 1998.

Malinowski, Bronislaw, *Myth in Primitive Psychology*. London: Routledge, 1926.

Merkur, Dan, *Psychoanalytic Approaches to Myth: Freud and the Freudians*. New York: Routledge, 2005.

Neumann, Erich, *The Great Mother: An Analysis of the Archetype*. Princeton University Press, 1991.

Veyne, Paul, *Did the Greeks Believe in Their Myths?* Chicago: University of Chicago Press, 1988.

STUDIES OF MYTHOLOGISTS AND MYTHOLOGICAL SCHOOLS

Ackerman, Robert, *The Myth and Ritual School: J. G. Frazer and the Cambridge Ritualists*. 2nd edn, New York and London: Routledge, 2002.

——, *J.G. Frazer, His Life and Work*. Cambridge University Press, 1987.

Beach, Edward Allen, *The Potencies of God(s): Schelling's Philosophy of Mythology*. Albany: SUNY Press, 1994.

Berlin, Isaiah, *Vico and Herder: Two Studies in the History of Ideas*. New York: Viking, 1976.

Brisson, Luc, *Plato the Myth Maker*. Gerard Naddaf (trans.). Chicago: University of Chicago Press, 1998.

Cannon, Garland, *The Life and Mind of Oriental Jones: Sir William Jones, the Father of Modern Linguistics*. Cambridge: Cambridge University Press, 1980.

Ellwood, Robert, *The Politics of Myth: A Study of C.G. Jung, Mircea Eliade, and Joseph Campbell*. Albany: SUNY Press, 1999

Rennie, Bryan S. *Reconstructing Eliade*. Albany: SUNY Press, 1996.

Segal, Robert A., *Joseph Campbell: An Introduction*. New York: Garland, 1987.

Strenski, Ivan, *Four Theories of Myth in Twentieth-Century History: Cassirer, Eliade, Lévi-Strauss, and Malinowski*. Iowa City: University of Iowa Press, 1987.

MODERN MYTH

Baum, L. Frank, *The Annotated Wizard of Oz*. Michael Patrick Hearn (ed. and annotator). New York: W. W. Norton, 2000.

——, *The Wonderful Wizard of Oz*. Chicago: Hill, 1900.

Curry, Patrick, *Defending Middle-earth: Tolkien, Myth, and Modernity*. New York: St Martin's Press, 1977.

Devine, Carole, *Star Trek Revealed: The Spiritual Dimension of the Original Series*. Virginia Beach, VA: Bruce and Bruce, 2007.

Galipeau, Steven A., *The Journey of Luke Skywalker: An Analysis of Modern Myth and Symbol*. Chicago: Open Court, 2001.

Henderson, Mary, *Star Wars: The Magic of Myth*. New York: Bantam Spectra, 1997.

Kraemer, Ross S., William Cassidy, and Susan L. Schwartz, *Religions of Star Trek*. Boulder, CO: Westview Press, 2001.

Tolkien, J. R. R., *The Lord of the Rings*: 3 parts; *The Fellowship of the Ring;*

The Two Towers; The Return of the King. London: Allen & Unwin, 1954–5.

———, *The Annotated Hobbit*. Annotated by Douglas A. Anderson. Revised edn, Boston: Houghto Mifflin, 2002.

———, *The Hobbit*. London: George Allen & Unwin, 1937.

INDEX

Made in the USA
Middletown, DE
23 August 2020

16026365R00106